PRAISE FOR *I WAS A FAT DRUNK CATHOLIC SCHOOL INSOMNIAC*

"Jamie Iredell is my favorite kind of essayist: Smart, interested in the world, and always willing to push past the received story to see the darker story where beauty lives. Most of all, essay by essay, he proves to be a good companion. My only complaint about *I Was a Fat Drunk Catholic School Insomniac* is that it ended too soon. I wanted it to go on and on."
—Kyle Minor, author of *Praying Drunk*

"About a third of the way through Jamie Iredell's *I Was a Fat Drunk Catholic School Insomniac*, I was content to be reading a collection of super-smart, hilarious, and honest essays. As the book progressed, though, what emerged was a compelling cumulative portrait of the artist, father, addict and husband as a young, thoughtful and passionate fuck-up. I love Iredell's words. I trust them. I'd let them take me anywhere."
—Chad Simpson, author of *Tell Everyone I Said Hi*

"Akin to Montaigne, Jamie maps the perennial stuff—fatness, racism, drugs, shopping, sex, heroes, politics, suicide, religion—by surveying his own soul. Jamie's an honest pilgrim, and American readers are lucky to have him."
—Ken Baumann, author of *Solip*

"Jamie Iredell takes the reader through varied, but united, territories of heartfelt memoir, social, political and anthropological explorations, and the writer's life. These essays constantly shift in form, tone, and in high and low language. Iredell is by turns funny, serious, irreverent, and learned. But what binds all of *IWAFDCSI* together is, to use a painterly term, Jamie's amazing palette—and Jamie can paint anything he damn well wants."

—Ruaun Klassnik, author of *The Moon's Jaw*

"*I Was a Fat Drunk Catholic School Insomniac* is Jamie Iredell in a glass-skinned body, except where veins and bones should be are neon coated flaws and all the beautifully disclosed imperfections of being. The honesty here is champion."

—J. A. Tyler, author of *Colony Collapse*

"Some nonfiction is like a representation of the writer's brain, some a representation of his heart. Jamie Iredell's is a representation of his humanity. These essays always remind you that behind the work is a person. This book is as human as it comes."

—Matthew Salesses, author of *I'm Not Saying, I'm Just Saying*

"Jamie Iredell impresses through his ability to shift from clever wordplay to smart social commentary to heartfelt moments with his daughter, and to do so with lyric control and emotional authenticity. The prose pulses with the strength of experience reconsidered. Readers will appreciate, and return to, this linguistic ride."

—Nick Ripatraxone, author of *This Darksome Burn*

"'Divide yourself among those things you love,' writes Jamie Iredell, and so he seems to have done. *I Was a Fat Drunk Catholic School Insomniac* dexterously divides itself into recovery narrative, occasional piece, review, and letter to the future, each essay more wonderful than the last, each genre revealing something new. And in the cracks and chasms between is an impressively honest inquiry into what it means to be and to have been Jamie Iredell."

—Gabriel Blackwell, author of *Critique of Pure Reason*

I Was a Fat Drunk Catholic School Insomniac

Jamie Iredell

I Was a Fat Drunk Catholic School Insomniac

© 2013 by Jamie Iredell

First Edition

All Rights Reserved

No part of this book may be reproduced without written permission of the publisher, except in reviews. Direct inquiries to:

Future Tense Books
P.O. Box 42416
Portland, OR 97242
www.futuretensebooks.com

I Was a Fat Drunk Catholic School Insomniac / Jamie Iredell. -- 1st ed.
   ISBN 978-1-892061-47-8 (hardcover : acid-free paper) — ISBN 978-1-892061-46-1 (pbk. : acid-free paper)

Many of these essays originally appeared, most in different form, in *HTMLGiant*, *The Good Men Project*, *The Nervous Breakdown*, *The Rumpus*, *Thought Catalog*, and *Sundog Lit*.

Cover Design by Bryan Coffelt

Printed in the United States of America

Also by Jamie Iredell

Prose. Poems. a Novel.
The Book of Freaks

I WAS A FAT DRUNK CATHOLIC SCHOOL INSOMNIAC

CONTENTS

Fat / 3

What Can Happen to You When You Read / 21

What Is a Jagger? / 35

What You Can Learn from LSD / 53

How to Not Get Arrested for Driving While High on Crack and After Having Drunk a Bunch of Vodka at a James Taylor Concert / 59

A Brief History of Opiate Use / 69

The Shape of Ideas / 77

Never Pay for a Cab this Way if You Can Help It / 85

One Way to Survive an Abusive Relationship / 91

13 Steps to Becoming a Barslut, and What Happens Afterwards / 101

The Most Disgusting Things I Did While I Was a Smoker / 107

What It's Really Like / 115

A Brief, Depressing, Hilarious, Disgusting History with Pickup Lines / 121

How Unattractive People Really Are / 129

The Gods of California and North Carolina Fistfight in Heaven / 135

Superheroes Are Our Parents, or, Our Parents Are Superheroes, or, A Review of Chronicle / 143

This Essay Cannot Sleep / 157

Where All the Good Guys Are / 171

Dear Kinsey, / 175

Acknowledgements / 197

For "America"

FAT

According to the average weight-height chart, I'm "obese": six feet tall and 250 pounds. I should be, according to these charts, somewhere between 140 and 180 pounds. I tell my wife this and her look askance suggests that either I am what they say and she's worried, or "they" are crazy. I think the latter is more likely, because if you were to ask my relatives, friends, and doctors throughout my history, I'm "big boned," "barrel-chested," "chubby," "chunky," "heavy," and "husky," but not "fat." But whatever "they" call it, I have been what I call "fat" all of my life.

I've also always been active and have not had abnormally bad eating habits. My parents were athletic, joggers, and they stressed the importance of exercise. Between the two of them they've completed seven marathons. My sister's finished two, just like my uncle on my mother's side. I started running regularly when I was fourteen. I've yet to tackle the marathon, but I've run plenty of 10Ks and 5Ks, and the farthest I've ever run at one time was I think nine miles. I played baseball, football, threw the discus in track and field, and even played a little youth league basketball. My brother was perhaps the most talented of us Iredells in team sports, as he stole bases off pitchers routinely, and Rickey Henderson was his idol. And my brother should have been such a good athlete: he's lanky and slender, all legs, and he highlights the difference in genetic dispersion among my siblings and me. Our sister occupies a kind of middle ground. In a family home video at the pool, circa 1985, my mother remarks to my father that my sister looks to be "getting a bit of a tummy," and she should "start jogging with Mommy." Before you get your hackles up about girls and body image, know that the same was suggested to me: in a photo I am about six years old, and I'm running down the street with my mother, in my own little "running outfit."

I'm still a jogger. I run between three and five miles per day, at least five days a week, and this seems to do nothing but ensure that I'm in relatively good athletic health, compared to even some of my skinnier friends. But I struggle—as I have since I became aware of my own body—with who I am and what social pressures and medical experts say I ought to be.

My frame and proportions and goatee make me look like a stereotypical motorcycle gang member, but I do not own a motorcycle and even included a clause about never riding one in my wedding vows (there's a whole other thing about my propensity to hurt myself that I won't get into here).

My "heaviness" has to be due, at least somewhat, to genetics. On my father's side my relatives are the clichéd tall, dark, and handsome—as I described my brother above. They're all limbs and abs and strong jaws and dark hair. On my mother's side it's a different story. My aunts are obese: squat and round, topping 250 pounds apiece. My mother, contrariwise, is very normal: five feet, five inches tall, and for most of her adult life she's probably been near 130 pounds. My uncle, my mother's brother—the one who has completed two marathons, and whom I most resemble—has a propensity toward chubbiness, and recently endured surgery to place a stent in one of his clogged coronary arteries.

Whether or not this family history had anything to do with it, my parents did not feed my siblings or me unhealthy foods. We learned the virtues of a healthy diet and lifestyle. We lived in California, birthplace of fad diets and the health food craze. I'm convinced this is one of my mother's reasons for salad-eating. I've heard Mom ask a server what salads the restaurant serves and she adds to this, "We're Californians," as if statehood explains why she would like a salad, as only Californians prefer such fare. Once, here in Atlanta, on a visit to famed BBQ restaurant Daddy D'z, my mother, glancing over the menu, queried our server regarding the lack of salads. The server, a woman I'd known for some years at this establishment, and with whose wry humor and unabashed coolness I'd become familiar, looked unsmiling at my mother and said, plainly, "You don't come here to get a salad." However, that salad-eating habit passed my way and it is a foodstuff I'm drawn to. Still, I suppose that my genetics, despite any salad-eating, are what they are, and I remain "husky," even if it's true that I have lost weight before, though that was only because I starved myself.

People always talk about the "obesity epidemic" and getting up off the couch and getting fit. It's like the First

Lady's social campaign, or something. And some brave women have talked about what it's like to be fat, but hardly anyone talks about what it's like for men. Recent Nike ads feature jogging fat kids—or try this: Google image search "plus-sized male models"—but still, there's little talk by fat guys about being fat guys, and hardly anything at all about fat guys working their fat asses off not to be fat.

Most fat people don't get that way out of nowhere; they've been fat for years. If I use my own case as one example: I have been fat since toddlerhood.

I'll never forget the first day of kindergarten, when I was afraid to leave my mother's side at the door to the classroom, and she pointed out the other children, already playing and learning and doing the things that kindergartners do. I found Ben Wellesly, and we became best friends in elementary school. One of the reasons for that—I know it to be true—was that he looked like me: same pudge, same chubby cheeks, same dirty blonde bowl-cut hair. Other elementary school kids would call us the Fat Boys, or the Chubby Duke Boys (since *The Dukes of Hazzard* was a popular show at the time, and we both routinely wore checked button-down shirts)—anything they could think of to make fun of us for our weight, and the fact that we chummed about at recess and lunch, a chubby duo.

I also cannot forget standing in assembly at this same elementary school to pledge allegiance to the American flag, and when I stumbled and stepped on another boy's foot and he said, "Watch it, fat ass." The shame and embarrassment that welled up in me must've made my chubby cheeks redder than they already were with the freckles that freckled them. I wanted nothing more at that moment than to go home to my mother who loved me, who would hug me to her and tell me that I was fine, that I would grow out of it.

My crushes on girls began in the second grade, and I cannot forget being shunned and unnoticed, knowing that I was undesirable (I admit that this is somewhat ridiculous, since I'm talking about the *second grade*, but it was there, a palpable feeling of non-inclusion). I remember my own parents, talking to my doctors with concern (rightly so), but also admonishing me for my heft, encouraging me to exercise more and more and more. And, yes, my parents were telling me to *exercise*, because exercise went beyond "play," this latter of which I did in abundance.

Then there were my siblings, both of them lean and tall, who also called me "fat" and "fat ass." I was not only larger, of course, but older and stronger, and I used my mass to my advantage, saying things like, "If you don't shut up I'll sit on you." But my siblings predictably turned this threat against me, making fun of the fact that my recourse to their teasing was to use my weight. And they ran faster than me, the skinny little shits.

Also, in the second grade a boy named OJ ran up to me on the playground, reached between my legs and squeezed my balls as hard as he could, and damn did that hurt. I don't think he did this for any reason other than he was mischievous (he was always sent to the principal's office, and had behavioral problems through to high school), and he made a sinister face at me while he squeezed and I gasped, and then he ran his skinny little ass away, far too quickly for my chubby legs to catch him.

I did have girlfriends, and I can safely say that—in retrospect—my lady luck has come as a result of overwhelming desire and perseverance despite my physical limitations. I'm not "hot," as everyone seems to describe it these days. I am freckled and hairy and fat and big and I drink a lot of beer. I'm like a Viking. But in the third grade there was a girl named Marisol whom I wanted to hug and whose hair I wanted to run my fingers through. I hadn't any clue about sex, but I knew I wanted these simple things and that was enough. My parents had bedside lamps that had cut-glass "crystals" that screwed in atop the lightbulbs, and this fixture I unscrewed and took to school, a sparkling gift to my Marisol. Marisol looked at this appliance-detached gift, from where she sat directly in front of me in our row at Castroville Elementary (Mrs. M's class), and she looked bewildered. She didn't know what this piece of glass was, or what she was supposed to do with it. I recall that she said thank you, but maybe she did not. Anyway, I have persevered and to this date I am successfully married and have produced offspring—proof that in life, at least from a Darwinian perspective, I am successful, even if I am fat.

In the fourth grade I migrated to a new school, a Catholic school in Salinas, twelve miles from the town in which I'd spent my previous elementary school years. I was the new kid, and I was white, and I was fat. I got made fun of for these things in reverse order: the first thing anyone noticed was my fatness; secondly my whiteness (most fellow-students were Mexican); thirdly, my newness. I spent the entire year at lunch and recess leaning against a pole at the edge of the yard in which the other children played.

Everyone farts, but it's like a cliché, or something, that fat people fart a lot. I once had to fart in the middle of class. This was no usual fart; I could do nothing to contain it, and my theory was that I could cover up the sound with my voice. We had read John Steinbeck's *The Pearl* and my teacher, Sister Martinez, asked for a student to describe the titular jewel. I leapt from my seat, arm in the air. I was called upon. I yelled my description, and since I was a dork it was probably something like, "A pearl is a piece of rock or silt that has invaded a mollusk and the oyster has coated the grain with layers and layers of calcium that makes it smooth and shiny," and throughout my loud explication I also emitted a continuous and enormous fart that no matter how loud or eruditely I talked could not be masked, and my classmates giggled. Sister Martinez tried not to, but did anyway. So you can understand that in the fourth grade, as often as was possible, I was sick or faked it so that I didn't have to keep going to school, and at the end of that year my parents agreed when they asked me if I'd be happier back at my original school, and I said yes.

Looking back at my experiences at that school where I thought I'd be happier, I see the extent of my appetites. The schools in Castroville were public schools and so had school lunch programs and cafeterias, but I was not on a school lunch program and my mom packed my lunch into a lunchbox that depicted *The Dukes of Hazzard*'s "General Lee" and assorted characters, and later, as I outgrew using that, plain brown paper sacks. And I remember the thermos-fulls of milk that came with those lunchboxes, and the lack thereof when I toted a sack lunch. The milk in those thermoses was beyond room temperature by lunchtime—not very refreshing, and not at all appetizing. I always wanted something cold to drink, something other than water, and those school lunch kids each received, as part of their lunch tray, a cup-sized carton of milk, and many of those kids never drank it. I could've bought my own milk for a quarter, and I often asked my mother for this allowance before school each day, and sometimes I fished it out of the jug my father kept atop his bedroom dresser for the change he dumped there. But, more often than not, there was no quarter in that change jug, and Mom hadn't one to give, and also she asked me what I needed the quarter for, when I had a thermos of milk already. I always asked. I never stole, or took the milk, and I never pawed it out of the trash like some bear cub. But I remember more than one boy, tired of me asking every day if he was going to drink his milk, pushing it to me across those cheap Formica-covered cafeteria tables, and saying, so that all his friends seated around him could hear it: "Just take it, and leave me alone. God! You ask every day!" And my face burned with shame at those times because I knew already that I was fat, and that this was an exhibition for these boys, because they laughed.

When I did get that quarter, it quickly cha-chinged up to two quarters. This was in the sack lunch era, when I would not have a thermos at all and Mom provided for said desired milk purchase. But, then at the morning recess when the lunch ladies provided more milk (plain and—*ooh, chocolate*), and some days tapioca pudding, some days donuts, some days cinnamon rolls, I wanted those, too. My begging a quarter from my parents got to the point where my mother gave me a talking-to, explaining that when I did that every day it was coming out to $2.50 each week, when my parents had already budgeted the week's groceries that were where? At home. And I was at school, I reasoned. "You don't need all that," my mother said. "It would do you some good to eat what we give you."

My father is a men's clothier and, due to my fatness, I grew out of the kids section at the local department store earlier than expected. Dad brought home jeans for me to try on, which he marked with chalk for the hem. What always happened, though, was that he asked me to put the jeans on, then he told me to turn around so he could examine the fit. Then he'd put his fingers in the waistband and tug to see how much room I had there, and sometimes he'd say something like, "Up to a 32 now," and this was what made me hate needing new clothes, and made me hate my father just a little bit.

I also hated going to the beach, which was inconvenient since that was where I lived, growing up as I did on California's central coast. It wasn't only baring my shirtless girth. My legs were chubby and rubbed together at the thighs, and when sand got up in there, well you can imagine: the chafing was awful. It was so bad once I had to walk with my legs spread as far apart as possible when we were leaving Sea Cliff Beach near Santa Cruz. We were walking the boardwalk back to the trail that wound up the cliffs to the parking lot, and some teenaged surfer dude passed me by and said, "You walk like you got a stick up your ass." I almost broke down bawling then. Dad was walking ahead of me, carrying the beach towels and cooler and whatever else we'd taken with us. I wonder if he heard that boy, and if he did why he didn't say anything. I remember complaining to him about the pain between my legs, but Dad was always stoic (when I was sick all those times in the fourth grade Dad would force me out of bed, saying "Just get up and brush your teeth and that'll make you feel better; you're not missing school") and he told me that I had to walk because he wasn't carrying me. I was too heavy for that. Maybe Dad hadn't heard that teenager. Or maybe he had, and he was walking ahead of me to distance himself from his walking-like-he's-got-a-stick-up-his-ass son, because my dad was embarrassed to be with me. Maybe.

Even with my parents encouraging me to keep a healthy diet the house was not without its entrapments. There is a sweet tooth gene buried somewhere along the strands of our DNA. There was a cookie jar, kept on the counter under the cupboards. Sometimes packages of individually wrapped cupcakes sat in the pantry. It was around this time, between fourth and fifth grade or thereabouts, that I stopped staying after school with Jeanie Larsen, the old woman who provided aftercare, and I began walking home from the bus stop on my own to a house without adults, for my parents would still be at work. And so those cookies and cupcakes sat there waiting for me and I would gather them up with glasses of milk (2%) to watch my Scooby-Doo and GI Joe and Transformers cartoons before I started my homework. Upon looking into the nutritional information for a single Little Debbie chocolate cupcake, I see that they are loaded with four and a half grams of saturated fat, eighteen grams of sugar, and six percent of the day's allowance of sodium. All packed into 180 calories. It wasn't uncommon for me to scarf down two or three of those suckers in an afternoon, and along with glasses of milk (at 122 calories a cup), my afternoon "snack" could easily be more than 600 calories.

By the sixth grade physical education was required, and one of the first things my PE teacher did that year was take all of the students' measurements. I waited in a terrifying line that ran out of the trailer that served as the

PE teachers' "office," set aside from the school's regular buildings, and butting up against the basketball courts, courts into which this line snaked, and I stood there for interminable minutes as my teacher called out each student's height and weight to a student assistant who recorded the info in a ledger. It's predictable, of course, what happened, and I knew it then: my turn came, and the PE teacher called out my height and weight, made no comment or face, and said nothing more, but my classmates got a giggle out of my 160 pounds. I turned red with embarrassment and left that trailer.

You can see that, with my parents' and PE teachers' exercise and insistence thereon to me and my siblings, their language (like my mother telling my father about my sister's "tummy," and my father telling me to watch what I eat because otherwise I'd get really fat, like *those* people [and here, wherever we were, he indicated said people as an example of what I could become and this example was someone morbidly obese] and I didn't want that to happen, did I?), and the temptation of foods that would assure not only the persistence of my chunk but contribute to its expansion, I developed the requisite shame that accompanies the carrying of extra weight, and this shame carried over into other emotions.

My fatness has propelled me to violence. Times when someone has uttered a "fat ass" or a "tubby" my way and all the pain and frustration and embarrassment I experienced in childhood welled back up again. As I've said, I'm not immobile, and I've hurt people: broke an arm once, nearly asphyxiated my brother, pummeled a frat boy, and once told a bum in a park in Midtown Atlanta, when I was jogging—my finger pointed inches from his nose—that if he didn't want the cops trying to identify his stinking homeless ass that he'd better just shut the fuck up.

When I was still a kid, older boys who lived in my neighborhood, teenaged boys who drove and rode in pickup trucks, who had greasy long hair, and who ollied on skateboards at the end of my street, called out to make fun of me as they passed me by in their pickup while I was walking home. I guess I'd had it with people calling me fat ass, so I threw a rock at their truck, with my aim meeting its mark. The brake lights flared up, the tires screeched, and teenage boys leapt from the pickup's bed and ran towards me. I was scared but defiant as they circled me. The driver was the kid who lived at the end of my street, and he had buck teeth and long, stringy hair that fell to his shoulders. He always wore a nylon parka vest, or a jean jacket plastered with heavy metal bands' patches. These boys shoved me around, and this kid with the teeth spat on me. They called me the typical: fatty, fatso, tubs, pussy. While they didn't beat me up, after that encounter I started carrying knives. And it happened again, just like the first time: those same kids drove past me on my walk home from the bus, and more insults hurled my way, and I hurled a rock back. I missed this time, but they had seen me do it, and they again jumped from the car to confront me, and this time I was ready. The looks on their faces when I pulled the hunting knife from my backpack: most of them just ran back to the pickup truck. That leader kid seemed stunned for a moment and didn't move. Maybe he didn't want to back away from a thirteen-year-old. But eventually he did, and the power it gave me was a drug.

In high school I grew taller and played football, which required more exercise than any sport I'd ever played. I lifted weights, and dated girls. I was popular. I didn't get into many fights. There was only the one, my freshman year, the fight where I broke the kid's arm. What caused the fight is beside the point, but in the course of smack-talking, this kid called me a "fat piece of shit," and some unbridled rage drove up from deep inside me, from all the years of being called fat by people I didn't know and by those who were closest to me, and I pushed this kid hard away from me and into a wooden fence post, hard enough to snap one of the bones in his forearm.

In high school I intimidated people, and friends said it was because I always looked pissed off. I've always been a brooder, not necessarily dwelling on bad thoughts, just thinking all the time, and that's what I did as I walked the halls from class to class, or to my group of friends at lunchtime. But in person I was friendly.

Due to my heft my football position was of course on the line. I was never good enough to be an all-leaguer, or even a starter. Some of that was due to my timidity. Whenever I got into a fight I was scared, just like I got scared when playing football, because the game's real violence occurs in what we called the trenches on the line. My line coach instructed me to pass block by getting the heels of my hands under the shoulder pads of my opponent, so that I could shove the pads up into said opponent's throat in order to choke him. On defense they taught me to punch my opponents' helmets near the earhole so I could "get their heads ringing," and knock them to the grass as I swam over them in my attempt to make the play. We cussed at each other across the line, made fun of each other's moms, and—of course—called one another fat ass. At least on the line, though, we were all pretty big boys. The sting of an insult is lost when the person insulting your physicality looks more or less like you.

While I ran and ran and ran and lifted and did innumerable exercises both while playing football and in the months leading up to the season to train for it, I never quite lost my gut.

In college I dated a woman who was probably bipolar, because she had very erratic periods of happiness, irrational anger, and depression. On top of that we were both drinking heavily. Anyway, when we got into fights one of her go-to insults was my weight. She knew that I had once slept with another girl long before my girlfriend was my girlfriend. This other girl was also on the heavy side, and my girlfriend, who was skinny, athletic, a rock climber, would say, "I can't believe you two fucked. That must've been quite a sight: both of you rubbing up on each other and grunting around." You can tell that she also had insane jealousy issues. She also called me fat and a fat ass, and when I threatened to leave her she said things like, "Good luck. You think you'll ever get a girl as good as me? Not with your fat ass. Who would want your fat ass?" And I *lived* with this woman. Once, as she berated me I begged her to stop yelling, literally on my knees, then the ground, as she stood over me in our kitchen and yelled insults and obscenities. When a friend happened by and rescued me, he took me to a bar, and we had beers and chicken wings and I felt much much better. Thanks, fried food and alcohol, and thanks friend, you who remain a friend even today.

I broke up with that girlfriend and moved to other side of the continent. For the first six months of my relocation I was depressed, missing my west coast friends and family, so I spent every day in a bar, drinking Pabst and Jägermeister and eating burgers and tater tots. By New Year's, when I looked at the family photos from Christmas, I realized that I'd blown up to the heaviest I'd ever been in my life. I had a visible double chin. I'd recently bought a new jacket, size 3X. I had not exercised in all that time. And, as times go, it was time for a change.

I starved myself, ingesting no more than one thousand calories a day. Morning: a bowl of Special K Red Berries with skim milk (196 calories). Lunch: one apple and one orange (157 calories). Dinner: a baked boneless, skinless chicken breast and a can of black beans or Bush's Vegetarian Baked Beans (620 calories). Each week I allowed myself one day when I could have whatever I wanted, and I allowed myself to drink alcohol. By the second week, when I went out for a big steak dinner, with a martini and glasses of wine, I couldn't get through even half the meal. In three months I lost forty pounds.

I leveled out: started eating a little more each day and began jogging again. I started to date women. But I still never got to what I would consider "skinny." And this is where I have to come clean and consider whether or not I have an eating disorder, body-image issues, both, or the potential thereof. Part of me wonders if I should have kept going with that lifestyle of less than a thousand calories a day. Would I have ever achieved what I think is "skinny," or would I have starved myself to death? Or am I addicted to bad food and exercise and the combination keeps me in this chubby state of limbo?

It doesn't matter. What matters is that I can't stand it when those closest to me laugh about my weight, or my eating habits, or other bodily functions, and that's probably a worse psychological condition. In a home video, watched at my grandmother's wake, we're eating a family dinner (looks like the Christmas prime rib), and I make a joke out of eating like I'm starving, shoveling the forkloads into my gaping maw. My brother, my childhood friend, even my wife, all laughed, said, *Jesus, Jamie.* And I was left burning inside, saying, "It was a joke." And everyone was all like, *Uh huh, a joke, right. You know you wanted to scarf down that meat slab.* Truth is, I *did* want to scarf down that meat slab, but I don't need you telling me that, because I already know, and apparently you do too, so let's all just shut the fuck up about it. But while I sound like I'm complaining about all these people who are close to me, I know it's not their fault. They really are poking fun at me, and I know they do this because they love me. I'm the one who's fat, and I'm the one who struggles with it, and that's no one else's problem but my own. Sometimes the requisite hurt that comes along with being fat has propelled me to drink, which of course packs the calories in, but makes me feel better. I know that I could lose probably twenty pounds quickly if I just stopped drinking alcohol. But I'm fat, not insane.

I mentioned my wife. We met, fell in love, married, reproduced. Here we are. I have a daughter now, and I think about those genetics of mine that I've poured into making her. My wife and I reiterate that we are committed to an active lifestyle and healthy foods. We try to get our one-year-old to eat as many fruits and vegetables as possible. But I can tell that the fruits are a lot easier, because the little one's got a sweet tooth.

I jogged four miles today. So far I have ingested a half a cup of nonfat Greek yogurt with about fifteen blueberries and a chicken salad sandwich. Dinner looks like it's going to be bean tacos. I'll probably have a couple beers, and with the last sips I'll take my Lisinopril for my high blood pressure. Already the results of my heaviness have crept in on my health, though I continue to battle. At least at my last checkup my blood pressure was so low the doctor thought I might be able to go off the medication completely. We'll see. My day is fairly routine. Nothing outrageous. Probably around a two thousand-calorie diet. There's a mirror on the sliding doors to the shower in my bathroom, directly opposite where I stand at the toilet to take a piss. It's impossible not to notice my profile. I poke and pull at my gut, trying to see what I might look like if I were skinnier. I wash my hands, return to my desk. It's like this every day. Part of being fat—or at least the kind of fat that I am, although I doubt that many other fatties haven't experienced this—is everyone else, especially your loved ones, telling you that you're *not* fat. Even my sister, when I mentioned that I wanted to write this, said, "But you're *not* fat; you're just *big*." Always "big," "big boned," "husky," "hefty," "barrel-chested," whatever. Maybe to them I'm really not fat, even if, to me, I am. But I'll rail against the "obese" label. I am fat, which implies the big, jolly, loveable guy I know that I am most of the time. Not the diseased, sick, addicted-to-an-unhealthy-lifestyle and poor-decision-making person that "obese" implies—even if I have and continue to display some of those characteristics. I've always been one who is great at lying to others, but likes to face the truth about himself. And that is that, plain and simply, I am fat, and I know that, and—I think, or at least I'm thinking right now—that's okay.

WHAT CAN HAPPEN TO YOU WHEN YOU READ

If you're like me your father told you and your brother and sister stories. They often involved characters named Jamie, and companions or equally relevant characters named after your siblings, and together they all tromped through forests and conquered giants and met and saved princesses and became princesses and princes and eventually kings and queens. This transpired while you were tucked under the covers of your childhood bed in the bedroom in which you grew up, situated in the northwest corner of the house in which your parents raised you. The covers covered your knees and, sometimes—during the scary parts when Jamie had to outlast ogres, dragons, or giant rats—the covers reared up to your chin, just as you'd imagine they might in a movie version of this story of your life.

Your mother and father read to you, too. Actual books. They read to you from the Little Golden Books, in particular your favorites *Peter and the Wolf*, *We Help Daddy*, *The Velveteen Rabbit*, *Baby Farm Animals*, and probably fifteen others that you cannot remember and cannot find or do not recognize on Google. By the time you entered first grade the texts were literally *Fun with Dick and Jane* because you were in school in the early 1980s and in your rural California public school district funds had not yet been directed towards updating the reading pedagogy texts beyond those in use since the 1940s. There were other early reading avenues, but most of these did not involve media beyond the actual written word. Your family had a television, as is/was requisite of any U.S. family. But, as these formative reading years occurred around 1980-1984, television was not yet the pervasive force it is today and your analog set had but thirteen channels, and there was no question of visual electronic media existing beyond these thirteen. Channel thirteen was the end of your televised universe. Channel nine was PBS, where you watched Big Bird and Oscar and Bert and Ernie as they reinforced what actual humans taught you about the Roman alphabet, and—as was your propensity, apparently—you largely ignored the vampiric Count. This would contribute to your later requiring a math tutor.

You read Dr. Seuss, of course. The staples: *Green Eggs and Ham*, *One Fish Two Fish Red Fish Blue Fish*. You don't remember reading anything like *Horton Hears a Who!* or *The Cat in the Hat*—anything they'd end up making into a feature film. You know you read *The Cat in the Hat*, but you can't remember anything from the book, except the image of a startled goldfish balanced precariously atop the upturned end of the Cat in the Hat's cane. Maybe Dr.

Seuss was where you first *heard* the language: its trills and snaking. Is that it, poet-boy? Speaking of poetry, you read Shel Silverstein, *Where the Sidewalk Ends*. Everyone else did, too. You read The Berenstain Bears without feeling smacked in the forehead by their didacticism. You read *The Tale of Peter Rabbit* and you were horrified—so, so scared—of Mr. McGregor. You also had, at home, *The Illustrated Children's Bible* by David Christie-Murray. You know you were Catholic—went to church every Sunday—but it's only now that you see how religious your early education really was. Despite this you also read, as many kids did, *Where the Wild Things Are*.

Eight years old, third grade, Mrs. Martineu. You kept your head down during multiplication table exams, cheating from the grid you'd written out, so small, slipped under the dittoed assignment reeking from the ditto ink. She had to have known, but never said anything (and this strategy worked, as through this cheating, by constantly checking those multiplication tables, you memorized them). She gave you that book, the one that opened everything: *The Lion, the Witch, and the Wardrobe*. You wouldn't read it until the fourth grade, that year you were so miserable, after you'd taken the entrance exam and had been accepted at Sacred Heart School and left your friends, who were all transitioning from Castroville Elementary to Gambetta. You always faked being sick, and sometimes you actually were. You got really sick, in fact. That's why you ended up having that ear operation, and all the subsequent ear operations you would have into high school to replace all the damage caused by the colesteatoma. But that year, the fourth grade, when you were nine, and you lay on the living room couch, laid up sick, you picked up *The Lion, the Witch, and the Wardrobe* and it was just like the cliché:

you couldn't put it down. You read the book in one afternoon. Then you read it again the same day. Then you read it again. The fourth grade, this miserable year, laid your reading foundations, because you did almost nothing else, your head bandaged, lying on the couch, book in hand.

And you read *Squanto and the Pilgrims* by A.M. Anderson. You loved this book, but in particular, you loved the first half of it, and would re-read that first half many times. That's because the second half of the book was so sad. Squanto is kidnapped by English traders/explorers, and taken to England where he becomes a slave to a wealthy English merchant. In London, Squanto learns some rudimentary English, and is—according to this book—treated well, even if he has to wear the hard leather and wooden-soled shoes that pinch his feet. But the bitch of it all is when Squanto's master agrees to send him home to North America. After the long sea voyage, and after all of Squanto's hope and happiness about returning home, he finds his village deserted, all of his friends and relatives dead from disease introduced years earlier—years during Squanto's absence. But Squanto lives on, befriends Miles Standish, and helps the early English colony—what we call the Pilgrims—to live in the wilderness of a place that would come to be called New England. But the first half of the book was the best part: during this time Squanto lives as an adolescent boy with his family in their village of Pawtuxet. Squanto prepares for his coming-of-age ritual in which he lives over the winter in the woods, in a shelter of his own making, and survives off food trapped in traps of his own making, and eventually kills a white wolf for its pelt, a pelt that another boy, a starving boy whom Squanto helps briefly to survive, steals before he leaves Squanto's shelter. When Squanto survives his ordeal, he returns to his village to find that the boy he helped has starved to death. When the boy's father finds his body, shrouded in the white wolf's skin, he proclaims his son a brave and victorious, but unlucky young man. This, of course, outrages Squanto, who complains to his own father that the boy had stolen his wolf's fur, after Squanto had helped the boy. But Squanto's wise father tells his son that what matters is that the other boy's father feels that his son did not die worthlessly, and that to disillusion him of this would be a worse crime. Anyway, the cool part you liked was all the survival shit that Squanto learns and endures, and how he came out, surviving the wilderness.

This ushered in a whole host of survivor stories, and of those that you remember best is *The Sign of the Beaver* by Elizabeth George Speare. In this book a boy and his father have built a cabin in the woods in 18th century Maine, which, at the time, would've been "the West." The boy's father leaves to return to Boston, where he'll retrieve the boy's mother and his infant sister, so that they can all live in their new wilderness homestead and live the American Dream, etc. After Dad leaves, this kid's got problem after problem. Some trapper dude shows up at his cabin one day and the boy, taught by his father to always be hospitable, invites the man to dinner, feeds him, gives him lodging, and upon waking finds that the trapper has cleaned him out. The boy's flour and salted meat are gone, so too his musket, that most important tool that would've ensured the kid's survival over the winter. After a series of mishaps in attempts to survive (trying to get honey from a bee's hive, for example, and you can imagine the outcome here), the boy, after glimpsing the Native Americans in the vicinity, meets and befriends a boy near his own age. The two become such close friends that the

Caucasian boy gets invited to the native boy's village. The boy learns how to make fishhooks carved from twigs, how to trap small animals for food, how to grow his own food, and he even learns the native language, and thus survives the winter. When the boy's father and his mother return (baby-less, as the infant had died), they're astonished to see that their son—whom they feared surely dead from starvation—thriving in his adopted wild home.

You also remember *Robinson Crusoe* from the Early Reader Series (No. 8), fully illustrated, and re-written from Defoe's original language, but with Defoe still credited as "author." You loved how Crusoe retrieved all that he could from the shipwreck that had stranded him on his island: hammers and nails and hatchets and guns, a bounty the likes of which most survival stories lack. Crusoe builds his island compound, befriends Friday, staves off cannibals and mutineers.

Maybe all these wilderness survival stories had something to do with your becoming a Boy Scout. What matters is that you read the Boy Scout Handbook and Scout Field Book, from which you learned various techniques for survival/camping in a number of ecosystems. This, you thought, was awesome. It might have been the first nonfiction (besides school textbooks) that you read for pleasure.

But mostly you read fiction: *The Indian in the Cupboard* by Lynne Reid Banks; *The Dollhouse Murders* by Betty Ren Wright; *Ramona Quimby, Age 8* by Beverly Cleary; *The Island of the Blue Dolphins* by Scott O'Dell (more survival narrative); *The Witch of Blackbird Pond* by Elizabeth George Speare. You blew through the rest of the Chronicles of Narnia books, none of them approximating the magic of *The Lion, the Witch, and the Wardrobe*. You wanted to live with Peter, Susan, Edmund, and Lucy all the time, and regretted the books that strayed from their storyline.

When your mom and dad ordered the World Book Encyclopedia it came with the accompanying Childcraft series encyclopedias, and you fingered through the text and images, your favorite the *World and Space* book, with the photo of the sun and of the tornado on the cover. This began your interest in science. You loved the cheap bright illustrations. You loved the *Arts and Crafts* text that taught you how to make a cockpit out of a TV box, in which you might play pilot, like your grandfather. You loved the part of the *World and Space* text that showed you the leaves and fruit and seeds of various trees, most of which weren't native to your part of California, but later—so much later—when you'd move east, you'd say "Sycamore" to the sycamore trees, when you spied their spiny seed pods fallen to the paths around the park in which you'd jog, the illustration of these pods from the *World and Space* children's encyclopedia burned into your memory.

When you started in at A of the adult World Book Encyclopedia, your brother and sister would leave the television on, creep in from the family room, through the kitchen, into the dining room, and peer around the entryway into the living room, to the couch, upon which you sat, reading. They spied on you as you were enraptured by everything you encountered: the Phoenician roots of the letter A (turn it on its side and it resembles an ox skull complete with horns), the aardvark, the abecedarian, Azores. You kept reading, even when you caught your brother and sister spying on you and they giggled and laughed, and yelled, "Nerd!" before getting up off their little kid knees and tromping back through the house to the room that housed the television. You remember how you never cared for that television. You could not hold it. It never filled your imagination the way words could.

You tried, but you weren't athletically talented. Not like your brother. He would run and slide, stealing bases in little league. He could juke and shoot, so basketball came naturally for him. Still you both read—and had your father read to you—from *Sports: Great Lives* by George Sullivan. You read about Babe Ruth scarfing down pancakes and knocking balls out of the park. You didn't know when you were young that even your brother would stop playing sports before he even got into high school, but when you're that young there are few heroes—outside of books—worth worshipping, and most of those you did came from the sports you so ineptly attempted to play. Underneath all that, at the end of the day, you returned to a book. When you couldn't sleep, flashlight on in your upper bunk in the night's dark: a book.

Your father subscribed to *National Geographic Magazine* and the collection stretched back to the 70s. Every issue was meticulously catalogued in leather cases, gold leaf-stamped with the appropriate date range to cover the issues therein. You pored over these magazines, scanning spines for articles that sounded interesting: "Life Returns to Mount St. Helens," "Africa's Elephants: Can They Survive?," "After an Empire...Portugal," "Ancient Bulgaria's Golden Treasures," "Titanic's Titan," "Reading Ape Bones."

In middle school the novels got more serious, or so it seemed. S.E. Hinton's *The Outsiders* hit you like *The Lion, the Witch, and the Wardrobe* did years earlier, and suddenly you wanted to be in a gang. Lucky (or not?) for you, there were plenty of gang members in Castroville, and some of them were the children of Norteños. You remember two boys distinctly: Antonio Hernandez and . . . Maybe they're not that distinct, since you don't remember the other boy's name, but what you do remember: he had XIV (the number affiliated with Norteños) tattooed on his forearm, and this kid was twelve years old. That kid once punched Mr. Bock—the algebra teacher—in the face when Mr. Bock tried to verbally discipline him. The other kid, Antonio, nicknamed Scarf for his scarred face, terrorized and befriended you. You even wrote a short story about Scarf. He died, stabbed and shot at a party in Salinas, in your freshman year of high school.

That last year of middle school, months before the earthquake that destroyed the Marina in San Francisco, though the quake's epicenter was merely fifteen miles from your house, you and your family visited England, and there you saw William Shakespeare's birthplace, where you bought leatherbound pocket-sized editions of his plays. You read *Macbeth* as your father struggled with shifting gears using his left hand and driving on the left side of the roads and highways. Though you had some trouble with the language, you knew at the beginning that there were witches, and that was enough to keep you reading. You read *Julius Ceasar*, *Twelfth Night*, *A Midsummer Night's Dream*. But you came home from abroad and both the San Francisco Giants and the Oakland A's were tearing it up, and you forgot about reading. Then came the World Series, and of course the earthquake.

Your freshman year you read Homer's *Odyssey*. You don't remember reading anything else. Around this time you started smoking pot, and that likely has something to do with your broken memory. Or maybe not, because in sophomore year, in Mr. Declan's English class, you read *Flowers for Algernon*, *Of Mice and Men*, *Death of a Salesman*,

The Crucible. And you were surprised with *Of Mice and Men* from its opening sentence: "A few miles south of Soledad, the Salinas River drops in close to the hillside bank and runs deep and green." You never knew that someone had written *books* about the place where you were from. Hereafter you'd read all things Steinbeck.

Junior year in AP English with Mrs. McAllister was all Shakespeare. You acted the plays out in class, reciting the lines, learning metaphor, the heroic couplet, the soliloquy. You remembered reading Shakespeare a few years back, and it was familiar, but you got so much more from it in high school, especially seeing other people along with yourself acting the tragedies, comedies, and histories. You learned about sonnets.

Senior year you read only *The Canterbury Tales* in Mr. Johnson's class. And I mean you read the whole thing in Middle English. Yeah, that's right, you learned Middle English, and you once thought Shakespeare was hard to understand.

What can happen to you if you're a reader is that you go to college, and that's where everything changes. You long since realized that any childhood dreams of being a professional athlete were just that: dreams. You took two classes that changed your life: Intro to Creative Writing Fiction/Poetry, and Western Traditions 203, where you read Jack Kerouac's *On the Road*. You didn't realize what a cliché that was at that time, and perhaps even if you had it wouldn't have mattered. Your mind was made up: you were going to be a writer—another sometime consequence of being a reader.

What does this decision bring you? Hunger. It brought you a new group of friends, other young people who likewise fancied themselves writers. It brought you some great joy those overcast days when you sat at your desk and banged out a story, pages and pages of notebooks filled with your awful rhymes and trite characters. Your Bukowski imitations. Oh, that's right: you were reading a lot, too. Hemingway, Fitzgerald, Woolf, and Wolfe, and all the other not-Kerouac Beats. You submitted to and did not win scholarships. You submitted to and did win scholarships. You published in your college literary journal. You worked crappy jobs to pay your rent: selling suits at Men's Wearhouse, making sandwiches in sandwich shops, pouring drinks in bars.

You thought: you know what would be a great idea? Graduate school. But you didn't apply to an MFA program; you stayed right there at your alma mater. This put you into a unique program: Literature and Environment. So you read Barry Lopez, Scott Russell Sanders, Terry Tempest Williams, Rick Bass. And of course you read everything, and I mean *everything* by Henry David Thoreau, Ralph Waldo Emerson, and Herman Melville. You realize at this point that you wish you could list everything you've ever read here in this essay, but you don't think that's possible, because you cannot remember every book, and reading something like that would not be at all interesting. The point is that reading brought you to this position, where you started teaching as a graduate assistant, and you had a grad assistant's stipend, which meant that, when you had to, you ate a lot of ramen, and sometimes you got your friends from the bar to comp you food. You walked a lot when your truck's battery died and wouldn't jump and you didn't have the money to buy a new one. One of the happiest mornings was the day you were walking to the university for your office hours and to teach and outside the old Harrah's Club in downtown Reno you saw, reached down, and picked up a stray ten-dollar bill fluttering on the sidewalk. And you had planned not to eat that day, and you weren't sure when you would eat again. What happens when you're a reader is that you're poor.

The other thing that happens when you're a reader is that you say, okay, I'm ready now: and you apply to MFAs and PhD.s in creative writing. When you were accepted you went. You moved across the country, far from your family and friends—and you thought you were poor in your old city. Your grad stipend was two thousand dollars less in your new city, and the cost of living higher. You said, *fuck*. So you spent a lot of time reading. Flannery O'Connor and Donald Barthelme and William Faulkner and John Donne. Man, did you fall in love with John Donne. Him and Barry Hannah. And James Baldwin. And Wallace Stevens. And you fell in love with Annie Dillard. And you fell in love again with Virginia Woolf. Let's sum things up by saying this was the most prolific reading period of your life and you loved all of it.

What happens when you're a reader is that you think back on all those survival stories you read, and you think about the times when you've had to survive in the wilderness: zero. Then you think abut all the times you've had to survive in society and it equals every day that you've ever lived, and reading was the survival tool that got you through it all.

What happens when you're a reader is that you have a kid. And when that kid's born, in her first half hour out of the womb, when she's but this squirmy jostled thing wrapped in a blanket and crying in your arms, you begin to tell her the story of poor Prince Hamlet, who couldn't decide. And she calms at the sound of your voice. And almost a year later, one night putting this little girl to bed, you pull out a book to read to her, one your mother brought from home when she visited last spring, and it's a children's book you forgot, but remembered once you saw the illustrations: *Hush Little Baby*. And you sing the words and show your little girl the pictures, *Papa's going to buy you a mockingbird*. And you tell this little baby *hush* so that she too can fall asleep. You begin teaching this girl at too early an age how to read, because you believe that it's never too early.

WHAT IS A JAGGER?

I grew up in the "Artichoke Center of the World." The homes that line the blocks and house Castroville's just-over-five-thousand-inhabitants cluster together like a raft that floats upon a green sea of artichokes. A mile to the west sit Salinas River State Beach's sand dunes, blasted by the Pacific Ocean's waves, and inland, over the slightly rolling hills, the artichoke fields carry to the foothills where they merge with strawberry fields and blend into the Gabilan Mountains, six miles to the east.

Though I grew up in it, I did not *live* in Castroville. Humans must work those artichoke fields. The humans who work the artichoke fields live in Castroville. Those humans are almost exclusively of the Hispanic ethnicity. I am white, and my parents did not work the artichoke fields. We lived in a housing development between these artichoke fields and the hills of the eastern mountains.

As all American children are required, I attended school, and there was no school in my housing development. My school sat amidst Castroville's tiny houses. My schools' (elementary, middle, and high school) demographics were Hispanic, White, and Other. Almost all of my classmates were Hispanic, the children who shared rooms in the one- or two-bedroom ranch-style homes that make up the raft that is Castroville awash in its artichoke sea. The other white kids lived near me, in my housing development, with their parents and their siblings, in the nearly-uniform three-bedroom, two-bath houses that sat on half-acre lots.

The school bus pulled into my neighborhood from Highway 156 and picked me up from where I waited at the curb under a two-hundred-year-old coast live oak, in a lot filled with golden brome. The bus then meandered the neighborhood's thoroughfare past my neighbors' gardened lawns and steep driveways to suck up the other children through the doors that yawned open. This neighborhood was not quite suburban, for there was no nearby "urbanity"; nor was it quite "rural" in the sense of a desolate wilderness road, or a dusty lane bordered by bucolic strawberry fields—although this did literally exist less than a mile away. And all of us white kids bussed into Castroville and met up with our Hispanic counterparts. There were, I think, two black kids and two Asians I went to school with.

These Hispanic classmates were, to be more specific, Mexican Americans. And it was not uncommon to hear racial slurs about Mexicans. In fact, more than once I'm ashamed to say these slurs ushered forth from my own mouth. From inside that school bus, or from inside my parents' station wagon, I and my white classmates, or I and my brother and sister, might laugh at a rusting and dented old Ford, its muddied wheel wells lowered to the tires, and the bumper sending up sparks when it hit a bump, all weighed down by the seven or eight field workers the vehicle carried. At some point—and I don't remember when we gained the vocabulary—we knew to say, "Check out those *jaggers*."

If you are like pretty much everyone else on the planet who is not from California's Central Coast you've likely never heard the word "jagger" used in this context before. A simple Google search brings up—no surprise here—countless websites devoted to Mick Jagger, and Jagger's Pizza, and the definition of "jagger," as in a jag, or something sharp that protrudes, like a thorn, and some Maroon 5 song called "Moves Like Jagger," the performance of which features Christina Aguilera (although Aguilera, due to her Puerto Rican ethnicity would not, technically, be a jagger). If you keep going through the pages on that Google search, by page seven, near the bottom, you'll come across the Urban Dictionary entry for "Jagger," which accurately defines the word I grew up knowing and using:

> 1) A Mexican person, [sic] that is straight out of Mexico. Ie. A first generation [sic].
> 2) A slang term used while talking to your friends. (If your [sic] Mexican.)
>
> 1) *Their house is jagger-like.*
> 2) *So I was talking to* [this] *jagger and she was like....*

But this "dictionary" definition of *jagger* is still lacking. Not to be outdone by other racial slurs, *jagger* is a complicated word, used in different ways by different people under different circumstances. It has a multitude of meanings and implications, some endearing and meant to signal belonging to a select group, some scornful, others mean.

I have taught the famous Gloria Naylor essay "The Meanings of a Word" many times. This essay explores the complications inherent in a complex word like *nigger*, demystifies its various uses, especially for the politically-corrected whites who might come across her essay. The unfortunate truth is, as David Foster Wallace has pointed out, that "some of the cultural and political realities of American life are . . . racially insensitive and elitist and offensive and unfair." That is our America. And I wish to demystify *jagger*, to express my regret for ever having used it pejoratively. Yet I also aim to show that, when you grow up on California's Central Coast, the word *jagger* becomes a part of you. I speak a word for Truth, and, to again quote Wallace: ". . .pussyfooting around these realities with euphemistic doublespeak is not only hypocritical but toxic to the project of ever actually changing them."

"Don't be such a jag."

"What a jagger . . ."

"Those fucking jaggers over on Axtell Street drive Pintos an' shit."

The above snatches of dialogue have been taken out of context, but demonstrate a few ways in which the word might be used. Jagger was used, of course, derisively, by both white and Hispanic people around the Central

Coast. The term meant different things to each group. White people, while talking to other white people, might talk about jaggers. They'd say something like, "Jesus, there are so many jaggers in Castroville," with a tone full of exasperation. Sometimes we'd even say our mass was held before the "jagger mass" at Our Lady of Refuge, because the Spanish language mass was held at 11 AM.

Mexicans who were truly jaggers (in this context) did not refer to themselves as jaggers. In fact, many of these Mexicans couldn't speak English well enough to form the hard "J" sound required to utter "jagger," and so did not say the word. They were usually darker-skinned Mexicans. Their sometimes lighter-skinned, more-fluent-in-English, more upwardly-mobile brethren, however, often talked about jaggers, calling the darker-skinned non-English-speaking Mexicans jaggers, as in the example above referring to "Those fucking jaggers over on Axtell Street . . ."

But Mexicans on the Central Coast did not always use jagger to demean someone. A Mexican might use the other dialogue examples cited above, usually when talking to a friend or relative. In these cases the word was used as a mild, loving, ribbing on someone. Example: My childhood friends Raquel Borona and Dani Martin might be getting ready for the high school dance that evening and while doing their hair, Raquel's waiting for Dani to finish using the hairdryer and in mock impatience says, "Why don't you finish already, jag," or, "Hey, jagger, you gonna use the hairdryer all night?"

This is, of course, not quite the same as Gloria Naylor's explication of the variety of uses for the word nigger. She says that "In the singular, the word was always applied to a man who had distinguished himself in some situation that brought . . . approval for his strength, intelligence, or drive," or "When used with a possessive adjective by a woman—'my nigger'—it became a term of endearment for her husband or boyfriend." No, jagger was always used as a put-down. But it was a different kind of insult when a white person used it when talking about a Mexican, than it was when two (or more) Mexican friends or relatives used it. In those cases jagger meant "I am a Mexican and you are a Mexican, and I can call you this because I love you and I'd like to use the hairdryer, too, please, so if you could hurry up and finish that would be great."

As a white kid growing up in this environment I somehow knew I wasn't supposed to call a Mexican a jagger to his face, that it was disrespectful and hurtful. From an early age my use of the word in this manner was relegated to only the worst kind of comeback in a bout of shit-talking, and almost surely precipitated a physical fight. One time this boy named Javier, who everyone called Javi for short, would not relinquish the marble I had rightfully won from him in a game of "keepsies." Javi was a big and tall Mexican boy and I was scared when he called me a "fucking *guero*." This—along with *gringo*—was the "pejorative" for a white person. I say "pejorative" because the literal translation for *guero* is "blond-haired guy," so it's not really an insult. But I was not such a small kid myself, and the social consequences of not reacting to the insult, and of not defending myself and getting the marble I had rightfully won were dire. I told Javi that he was "acting like a fucking jagger." Immediately thereafter we rolled around in the dust of the schoolyard's little corner where we'd set up to play our game until a third party stepped in before one of us hurt more than just feelings, and—luckily—before either of us got caught by a teacher and was suspended.

At the same time, I heard Mexican children use jagger to shit-talk other Mexican kids—Mexican kids who were not their friends or relatives. However, this was almost never followed by a fight. Imagine, as Antonio and Beto discuss the relative merits of the Garbage Pail Kids cards they're intent on trading with one another:

> Antonio: I'll trade you this Leaky Lindsay for that Phoney Lisa.
>
> Beto: Fuck that, eh. What you think, I'm a jagger?
>
> Antonio: You got two of them and you don't have no Leaky Lindsay.
>
> Beto: *Eeeeeeeee*, all right, eh. You're a fucking jagger already.

I do not remember adults using the word jagger, and I have never heard one say it since I was a kid. As per the examples above, as evident in the profusion of profanities, jagger was relegated to youth and, often, to gangbangers. The southern gangbangers called the northern gangbangers jaggers. The northern gangbangers said of the southern gangbangers, "Those scrap jagger *pendejos* better watch their ass."

There was a certain lilting rhythm to the vowels in the selections mentioned above, where they stood in for emphasis, as in, "*Eeeeeeeeee*, you're such a jagger, eh!" where "jagger" was pronounced like "dagger." Or, "Don't be such a j*a*g!", with the emphasis on the æ of *dʒæɡɛər*. This latter shortened version of my titular epithet was almost exclusively used as a term of endearment, saved for shit-talking from one Mexican-American friend to another. But the same word turned derisive when used as a put-down: "The Grijalvas are fucking jaggers. That's why they drive that fucked up Pinto." "Jagger" almost always meant someone on a lower rung of the socioeconomic ladder, or, when used to signal membership in the group of Mexican Americans, it meant solidarity, identity, while at the same time one Mexican friend telling another Mexican friend who was likely on the same socioeconomic level that, in a joking way, they were acting like they were lower class, but—just the same—*at least* they were Mexican too.

The Mexicans with whom I grew up expressed musical vowel sounds for emphasis in sentences. A long-breathed long E (i), especially, should enemies or friends utter insults: "*Eeeeeeee,* what he said!" You might think they sounded like a cartoon stereotype of a Mexican penciled by a white person, and, in fact, stereotypes come in their beginnings from places of truth. But these vowels came with a grammar. The short exasperated *Aye!* in an instant of pain or surprise. A longer, drawn out *Aiiiyyy* to signal frustration and annoyance or impatience. "*¡Aye me rompas el Corazon!*" "*¡Aiiiyyy, Jaime: esperate!*"

Of course, not all of the Mexicans in Castroville worked in the fields. On the south end of town sat big boxes for buildings: the packing warehouses. Some of my friends' parents were foremen and loaders and packers and forklift operators. Others were my teachers and school principals and the school secretaries and the butchers and produce people and checkout clerks at Fairway Supermarket and the pharmacists and checkout clerks at R&R Pharmacy and at Coast to Coast Hardware. But, on the whole, the agricultural industry supported Castroville. In the late 19th century the Union Pacific railroad selected Salinas—the much larger city ten miles to the south—over Castroville as a point of arrival and departure for passengers. Today only the freight trains rumble in to load up on crates full of artichokes bound for semis and boats in the Bay Area from whence they're transported across the nation and in some cases internationally. Despite Castroville's unsupported artichoke world-center claim, the vast majority of the world's artichokes come from Italy.

This is all meant to dispel the stereotypes I've pointed out, even if those stereotypes existed in great abundance in Castroville. The reality, though, is that Castroville houses a variety of people from different socioeconomic backgrounds, with different education and skill levels, and people of different kinds of ethnic mixes. Mexico is a diverse nation, composed of the descendants of native peoples, the descendants of the Spanish colonists who ruled the country for three hundred-plus years, the mestizo mix of these peoples, people of African descent, of French and Italian lineage. Gather these many different kinds of Mexicans together and transport them to the tiny coastal town of Castroville, California, present-day United States of America, and you can understand what Shirley Brice Heath meant when she referred to the "schizophrenia of being both Black and mainstream American." Simply revise that to Mexican and American. And do not forget that all of the people with whom I grew up were *American*.

Despite what sounds like my family's linguistic, racial, and geographical isolation from our Mexican compatriots, there was—as in such situations there is bound to be—integration. My parents' house was literally higher than Castroville and the Mexicans who lived there, by about fifteen feet of elevation—at a grand summit of 29 feet above sea level. Not only that, the housing development was called Oak Hills, and from our lofty Caucasian polis I could gaze down on the trodden peasants who worked the not-so-distant fields as I rode my bicycle on the bucolic oak-lined streets. But the center of our sociopolitical lives was Castroville. Oak Hills was simply a bundle of houses. There were no grocery stores or gas stations, no post offices and no schools. All such business was conducted in Castroville, where we moved among the Mexican people who lived in town.

At one point the parish changed the schedule of the English mass at Our Lady of Refuge so that the Spanish mass followed directly, and the townspeople were already gathered in front of the church, waiting, as we exited and congregated outside the large wooden doors of the vestibule's entryway. We shared a religion in Catholicism, even if some Sundays before we left my mother complained about the Mexicans standing outside and waiting for the Spanish language mass to begin. She'd say, "Can't they just wait for our mass to be over before they're crowding up the place?" Not even the sanctity of faith could dissolve the silt of racism. I never attended a Spanish mass, but I learned Spanish. Always having had a penchant for language in all its forms, I took to the trilled melodies my classmates and their parents sang to one another. It was a secret code, or a puzzle, to break and solve.

Because my school was predominantly Mexican I inevitably gained Mexican friends. Some days after school, instead of bussing three miles back to Oak Hills, I stayed in Castroville. I would amble the streets with my Mexican friends. We played baseball at the ballpark and bought baseball cards at Ken and Sons Produce. We ate french fries at Burger King. My friends invited me into their homes. Individual experiences have melded together in memory: a small living room with grandparents watching Spanish language television. Upon a shelf or in an alcove on one wall hung or sat a painting or a statuette of the Virgin of Guadalupe, and surrounding her candles and the withered black ends of spent matches. The homes consisted of two bedrooms, one for my friends' parents and another for the grandparents and what children might fit in that room, while the remaining children pulled out the sofa bed every night, or curled up under blankets on the floor.

Sometimes, my friends visited me in Oak Hills. More than once, one of them remarked that my family was rich. We had a three-bedroom, two-bathroom home, and a large yard. My parents had built a deck off the back of the house and outside their master bedroom's french doors was the hot tub.

Among my brother and sister and my Mexican friends was the Borona family and one of their children, Raquel, who, throughout her childhood and up till today, remains my sister's best friend, and a close friend to my family. I met Raquel when she was five years old, when my sister was the same age and they shared a kindergarten classroom. I played Little League baseball with Raquel's brother, Johnny, while their father, Bobby, was my coach. The day after Raquel broke up with her high school sweetheart, Frankie, I was there with my sister, in Raquel's apartment down the highway in Marina. And when Raquel cried and my sister held and hugged her, and told her it would be okay, I poured Raquel a glass of red wine and drove to Blockbuster and returned with *Men in Black* and a bag full of candy and the three of us laughed the rest of that sad night into memory. Last year, after Christmas, Raquel and her nephews, and my wife and I, went to my family's cabin in Squaw Valley, near Lake Tahoe, where I tossed the boys into the soft snow banks during our snowball fights. And this year, at Christmas, Raquel brought one of her handmade monkey hats for my infant daughter.

What I mean is, I have an intimate—nearly familial—relationship with Raquel. And, as it turns out, calling a Mexican a jagger when you're white isn't always an insult. When we were kids my brother and I made fun of our sister and Raquel (as brothers are wont to do): when Raquel came to our house we mimicked her accented Mexican English: "*Eeeeeee*, RaqUEL (where the emphasis landed), what's up, eh?" When Raquel and my sister said for us to shut up and leave them alone, my brother and I looked at each other in mock surprise and said, "Oooh, talking shit, eh. *Eeeeeeee*, what a bunch of jaggers, eh." And Raquel and my sister both could not help laughing.

I really had no room in which to talk shit. I had my own Mexican friends, and that, with my desire to learn the Spanish language, coupled with the social stigma of being white in a predominantly Mexican part of the world, made me wish I actually *was* Mexican. I moussed back my hair and donned long-sleeved pointed-collared shirts buttoned to my neck. I wore Z Cavaricci pants and black loafers. I drew cartoonish figures in sunglasses, with zootsuit chains dangling from their pants. I scribbled "Jaime de Castro" everywhere. I wished I could change my name's spelling permanently to "J-A-I-M-E". When we sparred verbally, Raquel came right back at me with an ironic, "What. Ever. *Jaime de Castro*." That always made both my brother and sister turn to shit-talking me for being such a wannabe white kid dork.

Today, I live in the southeastern United States, in what was once the center of this country's movement for social and political equality in the 1960s: Atlanta. When I moved to Atlanta, I found what I thought to be a diner up the street from my new apartment, but when I stopped in for lunch I found a Soul Food restaurant clinging to the then-gentrifying Midtown. It might have been my discomfort in my new surroundings (I mean, I'd never lived near so many black people in my life), and it could've been because of that process of gentrification, but the customers and employees of that establishment looked at me like someone recently escaped from the local sanitarium when I stepped inside one day after the lunch rush in the middle of the week.

In a movie there would have been a record playing, and the record would come to a scratching halt for no apparent reason attributable to physics. Whatever the cause for discomfort, I felt it when the thin black man behind the slit separating the front counter from the kitchen (there did not seem to be a clerk or any other employee working said counter) asked what I wanted and looked at me incredulously when I said, "A cheeseburger." The buffet had not appealed to me upon inspection, consisting as it did of fried chicken and a crusted tin of grits, and a likewise partially-crusted tin of collard greens, black eyed peas, and cornbread. Remember: I'd just moved from the west. In fact, I'd never once in my life seen grits. I don't think I'd ever even seen them in a movie, since you cannot see the actual grits in a film like *My Cousin Vinny*. Maybe nothing was happening at all. Maybe I was hyper-aware of my difference in that restaurant and the people working there were simply working, and tired, and had finished the lunch rush, and that cook just didn't want to cook me a burger when there was a perfectly good buffet just sitting there, and I could eat all I wanted, but I chose not to, and I was what you'd call a pain-in-the-ass customer.

The unfortunate truth is that there *is* that difference, there *was* that difference. In Atlanta there is de facto segregation. Black folks tend to live in certain neighborhoods and white folks in others. There are "black" and "white" business establishments, such as Dugans, the sports bar where black folks watch football on Ponce de Leon Avenue, which sits across the street from The Local, a white hipster kid bar. There are no Jim Crow laws enforcing any kind of segregation here, but this is the cultural norm.

There's a tendency to assume that racism in America is relegated to the pre-Civil-Rights-Act South, even though we all know that's complete horseshit. I never thought about the racism and segregation inherent in my own little fog-drenched pocket of the California coast, but as my wife likes to say, "There is no monopoly on racism."

Today there's this surge of anti-immigrant sentiment, racism masked by platitudes like, "We just think American citizens deserve American services, and that illegal aliens do not." And how do we know if someone is an illegal alien? Well, in Alabama and Arizona and Georgia and Indiana and South Carolina, apparently, the way to know is for a cop to stop someone they suspect of being an illegal alien and ask them for identification that proves they are in the United States legally. And just whom, do you think, might the predominantly-Caucasian cops "suspect" of being illegal? A blond-haired white guy like me? This sentiment in the United States is not new. I was there in California in 1994, when the movement to support Proposition 187 grew. This proposed California state law, passed that November nearly twenty years ago, wasn't all that different from Arizona's SB1070 from the more recent year of 2010. Prop 187 required state law enforcement to investigate suspected illegal aliens and request documentation proving their legal status in the state, and it cut off any funding whatsoever to children of illegal immigrants and would not allow them to attend school. I remember my friends—my legal Mexican American classmates—wearing T-shirts emblazoned with the Mexican flag. They waved the Mexican flag in our senior class photo, taken in the stands of the football stadium. Their parents advocated the boycott at school, when everyone stayed home. The law passed, was challenged in the federal courts, was overruled, and appeals dropped. All of the counties whose voters stood in opposition to Prop 187 centered on the Bay Area.

Historical irony: California has been one of the United States for 162 years. Alta California was part of the Mexican Estado de California, which included the contemporary Mexican states of Baja California Sur and Norte, for twenty-nine years. Nueva California was part of the viceroyalty of Nueva España, itself subject to the

Spanish Crown as a colony for fifty-two years. The native tribes that lived in what is today the State of California, the people of which—prior to contact—represented the densest and most culturally and linguistically diverse population of native peoples in all of North America, have been subject to the periodic visitations by Spanish, Russian, English, American, and Mexican explorers, and are still inundated by the settlers from these nationalities and their descendants who have never left: this a total of 472 years. It is, at the very least, hypocritical—never mind whatever other legal, anthropological, ethical, and social implications such thinking and legislation can and might have—to enact and enforce anti-immigration bills proposed in any of the individual states United of America. It's downright stupid to complain of Mexicans "infiltrating," or "invading," or "taking advantage of" a place where they've long already been, a place that is "home."

What I'm really attempting to point out here isn't how the word "jagger" can be used to insult and humiliate one group of people while at the same time it can be used by that very group of people to say, "I am part of this group and I am proud of it," and all of jagger's other manifestations. This is really about the plurality of human nature. To paraphrase Whitman: we are large; we contain multitudes. We can be rude, harsh, insulting, evil; we can be gentle, tender, magnanimous, beautiful. I found all of this in one little town and its environs, far from any real "city," surrounded as it was by the billions of thistle-y artichoke leaves that hemmed it in.

We still call Raquel a jagger, and she still calls me one, too. When I got home last September and Raquel came over for dinner, she walked in the front door, and just before coming in for a hug, said, "What's up, jagger?" And Raquel still makes fun of me in the old ways, calling me "Jaime de Castro." I am perpetually reminded of my wannabe-ness, my deep connection to the Mexican American extended family around me. Today, my sister sent me a text message telling me that she would call this weekend so that we could catch up. The message reads: *"Pinche hermano*, I'll call this weekend." And trust me when I tell you that I am as white as white can get, but I am from California's Central Coast. We are family. And so I *am* Jaime de Castro. All those years in Castroville, with the Reynas and the Boronas and the Padillas and the Ramoses and the Jimenezes, and there lived us Iredells set apart upon an oak-studded hill, looking down on the flat coastal plain that housed our Mexican friends. And all this time we considered ourselves Californians, and thought that we were above the racism of the South. *Dios mio*, how could we be racist? But it's there, built into the fabric of being an American. Or, as Heath wrote: the schizophrenia. I don't want to be an apologist, but it pervades all things; it is us. The Civil War is still us. And we still fight that war. Some of us still hope that this great experiment will not tear itself into tiny pieces of memory in the universe.

What You Can Learn from LSD, or, A Work of Art Takes More than Seven Seconds

It was early spring, buds of green leaves sprouting from trees that had been nothing but bark for three months. Gray snow had not yet melted in the shadows in Angel Alley where I lived in my apartment that was built into the basement of a large house, the foundation of which was set into a hill, so that I literally lived halfway underground, like something out of a fairytale.

This day off from work, and with no classes, after a couple cups of coffee, I sat at my desk and turned on the computer. This was fourteen years ago, and as a much younger person and writer I had these romantic notions tied to the Beats, with whom I was far too enamored. This, I don't think, is uncommon for young, male, writer-wannabes. I kept a bottle of Jack Daniels in that desk drawer and I pulled on it as my crappy lines of poetry came out and hardly ever got revised. You know, "first thought best thought" bullshit. When I found the little folded patch of tinfoil in the slot built to house pens and pencils, I remembered the three hits of acid I'd stored there and had one of those *why not?* moments before the tabs found my tongue.

Since I was young, I was also easily distracted, so when my friend Chris, who also lived in the alley, called to see if I wanted to have breakfast, I left the computer and my bad poems and met him at his Nissan pickup and we drove to Jack's Coffee Shop on Victorian Avenue in Sparks. This place was a cliché of a greasy spoon, complete with avocado vinyl booths and stained glass lamp shades covering the bulbs that hung overhead. We sawed chicken fried steaks smothered in white country sausage gravy into chewable cubes, along with over-easy eggs and hash browns, and I was just starting to feel the acid in my stomach, that nausea of anticipation that comes with hallucinogens. I'd neglected to say anything to Chris about the fact that I'd taken it, and decided I would not, even when he called me a pussy for not finishing my breakfast.

Chris was a friend I'd met in the dorms at the University of Nevada, and when we were freshmen he dyed his blonde hair black and lined his eyes with black liner and dusted the skin with black eye shadow and painted his fingernails black too, and he listened to Nick Cave and the Bad Seeds. I had just entered college and had come to the realization that in college—unlike in high school—no one cared what you looked like or how you acted or what music you listened to. That is, it didn't matter to anyone but to the frat boys who were technically in college but were intellectually and emotionally still fifteen. One day I will deal with the fact that I myself was in a fraternity, and I'll talk about how I am full of contradictions, but right now I'll focus on the fact that Chris was my friend, even if frat boys might have thought he was weird. Chris liked to talk, and in his Nissan or my Dodge he and I would drive around McCarran Boulevard, the road that circles Reno and Sparks like an enormous NASCAR track with traffic lights, and that's what we did: talk. That and we went through packs of Camels. Chris was one of my few friends who, although he knew that everyone called me Jamie, insisted on calling me by my birth certificate name of James. And this was among the things that I loved about him.

On this morning, after our breakfast, Chris asked what I had to do that day and when I said nothing we made a revolution on McCarran, and we talked about literature and existentialism, for we were taking those classes together at that time. And, speaking of nausea, that's one of the things we talked about: Jean Paul Sartre's novel titled after this unsettling physical experience one often feels at the onset of an acid trip. We talked about Roquentin's fascination with his hands and with his pipe, when his *nausea* sets in.

At the time, I didn't understand the damn book—and I didn't understand existentialism (which only now do I realize is kind of the point)—even though our philosophy professor, Dr. Piotr Hoffman, would call on us to answer his questions and referred to us where we sat together in those stadium seats as "the two philosophers."

Chris explained that what this moment, the onset of the nausea, represented in the case of the pipe was the realization of the artificiality of boundaries, that a pipe is a pipe and a hand is a hand only because those boundaries or distinctions are human, and this is, thus—in some ways—false. By this time we were sloping off the base of Mount Rose, where McCarran intersects with Skyline, and the road's lines coming toward us seemed to enter Chris's Nissan's cab and go through my eyeballs and my head and exit out of me and the truck's cab, like the neutrinos that I was not then aware of passing through us and everything, though without being seen at all.

I don't know how many laps Chris and I made around McCarran that day. We passed the Men's Wearhouse, where I worked selling suits when I wasn't taking classes—or acid. We passed Rattlesnake Mountain where, on occasion, I would decide I needed to exercise and I'd jog up this sagebrush-covered hill and watch the 727s land at the airport. We crossed over the Truckee River where it winds into a ravine and makes a northward curve for the desert where it drains into Pyramid Lake, from whence all of Lake Tahoe's water evaporates. Eventually, we hung a left onto Plumb Lane and drove into the Old Southwest and meandered the neighborhood, looking at the 1940s bungalows. Still we kept talking.

By day's end we had—of course—figured everything in the world out, as young men—boys, really, just twenty-one years old—think they're capable of doing, and we stopped at 7-Eleven for a twelve pack of Red Dog. This awful beer was like $6.49 for twelve bottles and under each cap there read something like "Born to be beautiful," and next to this an illustration of a bulldog's ugly mug, and Chris would twist these caps off and read whatever it said underneath, then yell, "Red Dog!" and take a powerful first swig. At this time Chris was a writer, too, and he read lots—would talk with fluency about Milan Kundera and Richard Ford and Garcia Marquez—and he wrote short stories. Later he would fall in love with Spanish, and would live a year in Bilbao, Spain, perfecting that language, a language in which he'd earn a Master's degree.

As we drove into the empty sage-covered hills on Mount Rose's flank, above the old neighborhood around Lakeshore Drive, we were talking about writing, about what it means to try to put fake people in a fake world that you mean to sound like the real world into words— the world Chris and I had driven through and parked upon, on a scrim of snow and ice and rabbitbrush, in a development still under construction though work had ceased for the winter and had not yet begun again. The skeletons of future houses stood upon their concrete foundations like gallows on an execution hill. Meantime the sun made its way down the Sierra to the west. And we watched this sunset go yellow to orange to pink to purple and I said, "A work of art takes more than seven seconds." Chris was drinking his beer and he pulled the bottle away and looked at me. He said, "Goddamn, James." And he thought that what I'd said was profound, that I'd uttered the greatest truth that either of us had uttered all day.

But I said, "I don't know, man. I'm just talking out my ass."

I still think neither of us knew what we were talking about because we were just kids—very impressionistic and dumb kids privileged with a college education—and we were learning about friendship and the world and who we were and who we would become. After an eight-year absence in my life, Chris is my friend again, though we're separated by almost 3,000 miles, so we cannot cruise McCarran and talk the way we used to. But if there's time we'll talk on the phone. Though there's never enough time. I'm a dad, a college professor. I've gotten fatter. Perhaps, for my health and for the sake of time I would otherwise spend with my daughter, it's a good thing that I cannot make laps around Reno smoking Camel cigarettes and drinking Red Dog. But fourteen years ago I was still learning, and of the things I learned that day, here is the one thing, besides the value of that friendship, that's important: maybe what I said *was* profound—even if it was kind of lame. I'd set out that morning to write, and did not accomplish even this meager task because I took acid and went to breakfast and talked with my friend for hours. I did not finish what I set out to write that day over the rest of that week or month, or that year. But fourteen years later, here I am, and maybe I'm finishing what I wanted to write that morning, but I didn't know that this was what I was supposed to write in the first place.

How To Not Get Arrested For Driving While High On Crack And After Having Drunk A Bunch Of Vodka At A James Taylor Concert

I had this buddy, Terrance, who was into Bukowski and porn in which women tied men's ballsacks to staircase banisters and made the men ass fuck them while moving as little and as much as possible at the same time, so as not to rip the ballsack from the male body but to also create/endure as much penetration/pain as possible.

Terrance wanted to co-write a screenplay with me once and we started with a clown atop a sand dune in the middle of the desert—for no reason, just because a clown on a sand dune sounded awesome—and other than that I remember a character called The Great Author. This was probably some brilliant-not-so-brilliant stuff.

Terrance and I once talked a girl into getting naked with us. Nothing else happened. We just kicked it in Terrance's apartment, drinking, smoking cigarettes, all of us naked. When we got tired, we put on our clothes again and the girl went home. But later, as you might expect, Terrance slept with her.

So, also as you might expect, when Terrance started smoking crack, I was right there with him, because I'm that kind of impressionable—or at least I was at this point in my life.

The first time I hit the pipe nothing happened. I remember the rock melting like an ice cube under the lighter's flame. I remember my fear. I thought, *I'm smoking crack*. Then: nothing. No high. Terrance got all geetered out and kept changing the CDs after having heard twenty-two seconds of one song then he'd hit the pipe again, and again. He kept offering it to me, but I figured it just wasn't going to happen. So that first hit was the last, for that night.

The second time I smoked crack, Terrace and I were at a mutual friend's house, the home of this married couple, as in a couple of crackheads—but you wouldn't think that if you saw them; on the surface they had their shit together like anyone who has his shit together. They kept a Yorkshire terrier and the house was immaculate. I don't think they employed a cleaning service, and I imagine that all they did was get high on this shit and clean clean clean.

This was in Reno in the 1990s, and speed was just starting to make its way in the world, especially in the high desert, and crack was on its way out, and coke and heroin hadn't yet had their early 2000s resurgence. Crack it was, and the casinos glittered from afar in the night, and nothing ever closed.

We were at this couple's house on Reno's south side, past the airport, and throughout the night planes screamed in directly overhead to land, past Rattlesnake Mountain, which was named such for reasons I don't want to know. Again, the crack melted like a bar of soap disappearing on fast-forward. It bubbled and hissed and steamed and I sucked it up. It tasted, even, a little like soap. Some kind of fucked chemical Ivory. Then it hit me.

As those who have experienced the crack high will tell you, trying to describe it is an exercise in futility, yet I'll try. Euphoria washed over me, a welling of good emotion, like I knew that something wonderful was about to happen and I just couldn't wait for whoever it was to bust through that door and Surprise! Happy Birthday! or whatever. My heart rate jumped. All those feelings lasted mere seconds. Then I broke out in a cold sweat. Nausea came next. I thought I would puke. Everything got spinny. Then just as quickly the nausea and spins went away, replaced with the overwhelming euphoria. It went like this, in cycles, for about a half an hour. I lay on this couple's front lawn, Terrance next to me, the wing lights of 727s trailing in as they landed at Reno Tahoe International, along with the roar of their engines, and the billions of stars that shone through past the city's casinos.

When the high subsided I met with another feeling I can barely describe. As messed up as the above experience sounds, I wanted it *again*. I craved it. That's crack. I'll maintain that the hardest thing I've ever had to quit was cigarettes, but I've never felt anything so powerful in its immediate tug. I don't know how much crack we smoked that night but nothing would ever approximate that initial high.

A few weeks later James Taylor played the Reno Hilton, a hotel-casino that once hosted an outdoor summer concert series; today this hotel-casino is called the Grand Sierra. Terrance and I stood in the stands and passed joints and sucked down seven-dollar Cape Cods. The night came on, with the sunset fading away, like something out of a—well—like something out of a James Taylor song. I got pretty buzzed.

I'd driven us to the concert in my Dodge pickup. I knew we'd be partying, so I'd parked blocks away, in a neighborhood far from where I suspected the police might be lurking for drunk-and-driving concertgoers. Also, I knew and had known for at least two weeks that I had a headlight out. You can see where this is going.

But that's not it—or at least, not *only*. We left the concert after the last song—"Mexico"—and, no I'm not ashamed to say that I actually *like* James Taylor, and we walked these thirteen or fourteen blocks to my truck, and once we got there, we decided to revisit our married couple friends with the crack habit, for we were forming our own crack habits to accompany theirs.

An hour later, the buzz I'd felt from the vodka had been replaced with the rush of crack. And not only had we smoked a grip at this couple's house, but we'd walked out of there holding our own little inch-by-inch square baggies filled with rocks for later. It was going to be one hell of a night.

I kept off Virginia Street and any other main roads, and meandered through the neighborhoods, as we made our way from Reno's south side up to the Lakeside neighborhood where Terrance lived, where we planned to keep the party going. It was when I came to a four-way intersection that I met the cop coming at me, from the opposite direction.

I knew the headlight was out, and here's the thing about crack (and many other drugs, for that matter): It makes you hyper-aware of everything, especially whatever faults you might have, or those that might affect your situation. I know that this is a false sense of security; it's more like paranoia. It's more likely that in this hyper-awareness a crackhead's missing eighteen things for the one thing he manages to cover, but still. I knew I had that headlight out, and once the cop and I both accelerated through that intersection, I kept my eyes on my rearview. When I saw the cop's brake lights go up, I knew he was turning around and coming after my ass. It was a Friday. Post-concert. Prime DUI time.

I immediately turned into an apartment complex, drove around the back, and parked, and when Terrance and I got out of the truck, I ditched the keys in a bush, and we chilled out for about a half an hour, sitting on the steps that led to whoever might have lived at this place. Had you lived at this apartment building in the mid 1990s, and had you stepped outside your apartment at this time, you'd have come across two young dudes smoking cigarettes, hopped up on crack, sitting on your steps in front of your apartment, scared, and trying to keep from going to jail.

After this half-hour passed, I dug around in the leaves and dirt under the bush into which I'd tossed my keys, and once I found and retrieved them, we kept on our way, thinking we'd outsmarted that cop.

Of course, a couple blocks later we came across the cop again. It must've been the same cop; I don't know how there could be that many cruisers out and in the same neighborhood. But this time I was turning right, and the cop pulled up to the intersection (me with my blinker already on) and he was at my left, heading in the direction in which I planned to turn.

Perhaps it was at that moment, or maybe it was after, when I'd already turned and the rollers lit up when the cop pulled me over, I made up my mind: I was going to jail, and there was nothing I could do to stop that. A strange tranquility overcame me. My nerves relaxed. My heart rate slowed. I stopped sweating. I decided that there was no point in arguing with the officer, that I was simply going to cooperate. I wasn't going to tell the *truth*. I wasn't that dumb. But I wasn't going to be a pain in the ass, either. The plastic steering wheel in my hand, the streetlights. Terrance at my side, breathing heavy and saying, *fuck, fuck, the fucking cops, the fucking cops, man.* And I was cool. I just cooled out.

My window was already rolled down, license and registration in-hand, when the officer stepped forward, flashlight shining. He said he'd pulled me over for the missing headlight. I lied: "Yes, I realized that just this evening." I needed to get that fixed, etcetera. The officer asked if I'd been drinking. *Well . . .* I lied. I said that, yes, we'd been to the James Taylor concert, and I'd had a couple drinks. How many? the cop wanted to know. I said two, but it'd been more like seven—and then there was the weed and, of course, the crack just after, and the crack nestled in its baggy in my pocket as I sat there in the driver's seat talking to the cop at this exact moment.

There were two of them. They asked us to step out of the car. One cop talked to Terrance and the other talked to me. I can only begin to explain how sober I felt. It was like the tranquility that had washed over me had overtaken the turbulence of the cops' presence, of being high, of the missing headlight—everything—and I simply knew, was absolutely convinced—that I was going to jail, and I knew not to fight it, and I was calm. The cop pulled me to the curb and asked me questions, shined his flashlight in my eyes. He never gave me the stereotypical field sobriety tests. All he asked me to do was follow his pen as he waved it slowly in front of my face. The cop who was talking to Terrance kept to Terrance and never talked to me.

The cops retired to their cop car where they talked for god knows how long, but it was the interminable amount of time that cops take in doing such things. All I know is that they left me and Terrance standing there, kind of leaning against a fence that butted up against the sidewalk next to the curb where I'd pulled over when the cops' lights came up. Terrance and I didn't talk to each other.

Finally, the officer who questioned me returned. He pulled me aside, returning my license and registration. He said, "You seem perfectly fine to me, but my partner's a little concerned about your buddy there. His eyes are dilated and his heart rate's up, he's sweating. What's going on?"

I said, "He's been arrested before, so I think he just doesn't like cops very much." This was all true, or at least true from the stories Terrance had told me. I didn't have to mention the fact that he might have dilated pupils from crack, that his heart rate might be accelerated from crack, that he was sweating because he's high on crack—not that I would have, but I didn't have to lie. And, chances are, if Terrance did in fact have a record (something I did not then know for sure) and I acknowledged this when the cop asked me, he probably thought I was telling the truth, which I suppose in a certain way I was. Because the cop, my cop, considered what I said, just like you might imagine a cop in a television show would consider it: he turned his head slightly, flashlight-in-hand, and thought. Then he said, "I can understand that. Get home and get off the roads tonight, and don't drive anymore till you get that headlight fixed."

And that was that. Terrance and I got back to Terrance's apartment, and we got high again, and we smoked all the crack we had that night and I think we listened to a lot of the Beatles' *White Album* and to a lot of Al Green. I'd like to tell you that, while listening to the Beatles I thought deeply about what had just happened to me and all the stupid things I'd done: how I could've killed someone while driving all messed up, and how it would've been safer had those cops arrested us. I'd like to say that I learned something that night because of how close I came to going to jail. But I didn't learn anything that night. It's only now that I realize I was a fucking idiot, and I'm just lucky that I never hurt anyone, or myself. God knows there's some statistic out there for how often you'll get pulled over and arrested for how many times you drive while under the influence, but I wasn't thinking about any of that at the time. And I continued to drive under the influence of lots of drugs and alcohol for many years. But I don't think I'm telling you anything you don't already know. What I can tell you is what I felt that night, and what I felt later, and how I feel now: I wasn't going to jail, and I wasn't hanging out with Terrance much more after that night, because I figured I was done with this crack shit. Today I know I was lucky to get out of doing that drug and others like it with all of my parts in place. Terrance, he got really bad on it, and he lost some teeth.

A Brief History of Opiate Use

The history is long, perhaps exhausting, so to be succinct:

In the fourth grade I got cholesteatoma, which is a growth that ruptures your eardrum and oozes out this cheeselike substance that stinks like cheese, and the growth eats away at your hearing bones—those parts that resonate, the stirrup, the anvil, the hammer—and so I had surgeries to remove and replace these bones, which meant they cut me open. My mom, knowing I loved the Civil War, said, "You'll be like a veteran, with his head all bandaged up." The painkillers were Vicodin, and I did not abuse them because I did not know what abuse was.

Then I had my wisdom teeth removed and I tore my cartilage playing football in high school and I had seven more operations on my ears and through all this I took painkillers but I hardly used them at all except for how they were prescribed.

I worked at a pizza place that served beer and wine in Reno, Nevada while I was finishing up my Bachelor's degree at the university in that city. By this time I'd already smoked and sold a lot of pot and had taken too many acid and mushroom trips to count. What this meant was that I fit right in with my coworkers at The Pub. We proudly called ourselves Loadies, for we got loaded, and it didn't matter on what. We weren't particular.

It was with my friends and coworkers at The Pub that I first took morphine. Chris scored a few thirty-milligram pills and we each washed one down with Budweiser. We kept drinking through the night and the morphine crept in and made for this light, float-y high. My head felt warm and the muscles in my arms went loose. We kept drinking, sitting at a round table covered in a red and white checkered plastic tablecloth. A fire burned in the fireplace and on the big screen the Wolfpack sent three-pointers into the flapping net. Our laughter got so infectious that at one point my side stitch almost made me puke. Bob kept calling us faggots.

After we quit our jobs at The Pub we remained friends, and we still hung out at The Pub, where Bob still bartended, and where we drank. Sometimes Bob would sling us a free pitcher. We'd make our own pizzas in the kitchen so long as the owner wasn't there.

Mike came back from Burning Man with some tar. We were at Travis's house for a barbecue and for horseshoe tossing. The sun beat down on the dirt and sagebrush in the yard. Mike and I went behind the house and chased the melting black down a strip of foil. Sometimes the emptied cylinder from the ballpoint we used to suck up the smoke got a little too close to the sticky heroin and the drugs clung to the end and the plastic melted a bit and we inhaled the plastic's fumes. When I needed a second hit, Mike gave up the foil, and in the bathroom I accidentally dropped the pinch I'd pinched off. I crawled around on the floor picking up bits of dirt till I found it.

Timmy got a job at a café in Squaw Valley, near Lake Tahoe, where in the summer mountain bikers biked down the mountains and in the winter skiers skied. There Timmy met another employee, Tom, a guy who shot smack. Sometimes we couldn't get the real stuff and Tom sold us methadose. During winter Tom worked Ski Patrol, which tells you something about the people who are supposed to be responsible for your life upon mountainous terrain. Tom always wore sunglasses, even inside his dingy apartment where he never pulled the drapes open. His skin looked rough and red and he appeared to be over forty-five or fifty years old, but I think he was in his late 20s. Once I stayed in Reno, lounging around Timmy's apartment while Timmy himself went to work at Squaw. There I lay on the couch, got high, and watched Girls Gone Wild DVDs. I didn't even get aroused; I just watched these girls get talked into showing the cameramen their bodies. It felt anthropological. In Timmy's bedroom I found a box in the closet and in the box was a carton of individually-packaged needles, a bag of cotton balls, and a couple of fire-darkened spoons. I set about getting ready to shoot up, even though I'd never done it before and had only seen it done in movies or had a doctor stick me with the needles that doctors used.

I pinched off about the same amount of tar that I might smoke in a hit, and I mixed that with tap water. I was surprised at how water-soluble the heroin was. I heated up the dose in one of the spoons and tried wrapping a shoelace around my bicep to find the vein. Ultimately, though, I was too pussy to mainline it and I ended up shoving the needle into my thigh. I pushed the drugs in slowly. I was still surprised at the speed with which I got high, even though it had not gone directly into a vein. Turns out, it was a good thing, because if I'd tried dosing the same as I smoked I'd have been one dead kid. Instead, the high came in waves, felt like waves, too, like a rush of warm coursing over my face, like a beautiful girl stood before me while I sat on the couch, and she softly blew a stream of gentle breaths over my head.

One time I was with Bob at the Cal-Neva downtown and we sat at the bar and ordered Budweisers. I had already gotten so high that I was sick to my stomach, and I nursed a couple sips off that beer then gave it to Bob. I said that I didn't feel very good. Bob looked at me weird, called me a faggot. The cigarette smoke got to me, too. And this, ultimately, would be why I would stop using opiates: I liked drinking beer. I liked hanging out at bars by myself or with Bob, Bob who never did heroin and never would. But at that moment all I wanted was to go home and be alone with my high and the sickness that came with it, and wanting to do that I knew was not very cool and certainly not fun. So I would quit using those drugs, but it would take a few years and a couple thousand miles first.

Once, while with Moses and Rivera, in Oakland, California, in a cheap hotel room near the airport, Moses and Rivera were trying to hook up with a couple of college girls, neither of whom were interested in me, so I was bored and got the keys to the truck from Rivera. I knew that in the truck's lockbox sat a bottle of oxycodone that was meant for the day after this night of drinking. It was to be the hangover cure. There were three pills in there: one for each of us. I took them all. Back in the hotel room, where everyone had passed out, I turned on Discovery Channel and felt the high come on then start to nod me out. I got terrible hiccups that wouldn't go away. I kept trying to hold my breath but nothing worked. On screen, sharks leapt from frothy water with seals clenched between their jaws. I knew that it might not be a good idea if I passed out. I dropped my sternum onto a chair's back—my full weight—forcing the air out of my lungs. This kept me awake, and eventually made the hiccups stop. The next morning, with all of our terrible hangovers, Moses and Rivera were furious. The whole car ride they kept saying *Fucking Jamie* over and over. My chest and stomach were bruised from where I dropped myself repeatedly on the chair's back. My throat hurt terribly, too, but I don't know why.

The strangest, and the worst, though, was at my grandparents' house. My grandfather was dying and I drove into the Napa Valley from Reno to see him. I smoked some heroin before I got on the road, and I stopped in Colfax to smoke some more. I stopped again, this time in the parking lot of the park that sat in the vineyards just down the street from my grandparents' house, the park where they would take me and my little brother and sister when we were kids so that we could clamber over the jungle gym. I watched the children from the driver's side of my pickup as I readied my drugs, and they played, swinging on the tire swing that I too had swung upon years earlier. Then I sucked up the smoke from off the tinfoil and there went the last of my tar.

At my grandparents' house the scene was pretty bad. My grandfather was bedridden and he'd gotten so skinny that when my aunt (who was a nurse) asked me to help her by carrying him into another room where she could clean and apply medicine to his bedsore, I was surprised by how light he was in my arms. He curled up against me like a baby. His Parkinson's made him a prisoner who hardly moved and rarely made any sounds. I laid him upon the bed, and my aunt turned him on his side and asked that I hold him there and try to comfort him while she worked. She said, "It's so deep you can see his tailbone." She said, "I'll be very fast, papa." Then my grandfather did make sounds, and even talk. He gripped my hand, and his voice was weak, but insistent, as he moaned, "Oh, god, oh god, it hurts."

I cried. I couldn't help it. He was once the kind of grandfather who taught me how to take off an engine's intake manifold and how to shoot a rifle.

After my aunt had dressed his sore she asked me to go to the kitchen, to the refrigerator where the pain medication was. In the fridge sat a cup, and inside the cup sat prepped rigs, six or seven of them, full of morphine. I looked at those syringes and I had the strangest thoughts and feelings rush over and through me all at once. I wanted those drugs. Mine were gone, and I would be there at my grandparents' house for two more days with no way to score more. But I knew that my aunt would notice if some went missing. At the same time, this thought came to me without any hesitation: I wanted to inject my grandfather with all of those syringes at once. I didn't want him squeezing my hand and moaning *oh god oh god it hurts* ever again. I wanted him to die, and to die feeling good, so that he would not have to feel any more of that pain. But instead I took a single syringe to my aunt, and I left the room before she gave my grandfather the dose. I walked outside and in the vineyards I watched the sun set, and I cried and kept crying, though I'm not sure—of the many possibilities—what I was crying about.

THE SHAPE OF IDEAS

I met J at the University of Nevada, outside the English Department on a winter day, the cottonwoods of the quad leafless, as J cupped his palms around his cigarette to light it and I bummed that light off him.

He took philosophy and literature classes. He wore glasses and a goatee. He was bookish and handsome. His voice was butter, silky and drawn out. He'd say "all right," like "aaaalllll riiiiiiiight," maybe like someone like The Fonz would say it, except J could say this better than The Fonz because there was no affect. He was J being J as J was.

On the steps of Frandsen Humanities—the English Department—there sat a giant concrete urn-like pot and J and I would smoke beside it between classes and we talked about Hegel and Nietzsche and *The Lord of the Rings* and Faulkner, all of which J loved.

He got me my job at the Pub, where I met many of my friends, people who are still my friends today. I guess he didn't *get* me the job, but when I asked he said that was where he worked, and the idea that I might work there too got into my head, for it seemed like a far more fun job than selling suits at the Men's Wearhouse, which was what I was doing at the time. I'd have to finish classes, change from my t-shirt and jeans, shower, and dress in a suit or sport coat and slacks, with a shirt and tie, and tell people that our suits were the best bargain they could find anywhere in town, and I figured the Pub was an easier sell, convincing people to get another pitcher, or to order a large pizza, or to enjoy the turkey sandwich I made for them.

One time at the Pub, J found a baggie full of pot in the backyard when he was taking out the trash and when he came back inside he held up the baggie, shaking it, and said, "Anyone want to get hiiiiiiiggghhhh?" in that way that he had, and Leadawn, the woman who was our manager and whom we knew was a druggie even if she tried to hide it from us (because both she and her brother were obvious tweekers, and meth had popped up and become a problem across the west at the time and sometimes we'd drive past Leadawn's house on Ralston Street and the lights were on at 4 AM and we knew she wasn't out drinking because that's why we were driving by in the first place), and she was bent behind the bar storing glasses and she popped up and said, "I do," and J, who hadn't known that our manager was even back there, just started laughing as he packed the first bowl.

J had a girlfriend named Tiffany, a smart and cute petite brunette. Though things didn't work out between them, they went out for two or three years, lived together, and I think Tiffany always loved him and always will.

And I could see why Tiffany loved J, because he was handsome and well-built, with broad shoulders and a slender waist, sharp features, but soft, sad-looking eyes behind his glasses. He was mellow. He never got animated or excited. I only saw him yelling maybe when the Seahawks or the Mariners were losing a game on television—so I guess I saw him yell a lot. And J was a cook at the Pub, which, as a college hang-out, attracted all the girls, and Tiffany could claim J as her own, and she could also claim the free pizzas and beers that came with dating a guy who worked at the Pub, and also J was smart and caring, a genuinely good guy, and he cared for Tiffany, and I know this because I saw it.

All this gentleness, and J was perhaps the best fighter I've ever known. I've seen many a good fight, bar brawls (seriously, like fifty people all fighting in the Pub), but I've never seen anyone get pummeled the way J could pummel a fool. This one time at the Little Waldorf Saloon the guy J beat up was yoked, and had a shaved head—turned out he was a Marine. The fight started because this Marine guy told our friend and coworker Sara *fuck you*, after she refused his advances, and J heard him. All I know is that before the bouncers rushed in and separated us and them out, J was crouched like some fighter in a movie, and he worked jabs, left and right, kept his face and his glasses covered with his forearms when he wasn't throwing a punch, which was for these brief flashes, because the punches kept coming. And that baldheaded Marine, he was crouched there, too, trying to get in a shot, but failing, till he fell, and then the bouncers had us all in full nelsons and they dragged us out to the parking lot.

J didn't always protect his glasses. One time, at Chewy and Jugs, he took his glasses off when the fight started, and after we got kicked out he had to go back for the glasses the next day and someone had taken a nail, or something, and etched "F-A-G-G-O-T" backwards on one of the lenses, so it would be like J would read "faggot" when he had the glasses on. J couldn't afford new glasses and he wore those, with "faggot" written like that on them, for a few months, not that J cared, because he did not—not about the pejorative, nor about his mangled glasses.

The whole family was great, the Joyners. J's older brother, Tom, lived in Reno and was a big soccer fan, Manchester United and all that. In fact, all the Joyners were soccer fans, as Tom and J had both excelled at the sport when they were in high school in Winnemucca, Nevada. Tom lived with his longtime girlfriend on Barker Circle, off of 7th Street. J's little brother, Bill, came into town from Winnemucca after high school (where their parents still lived) and soon he, too, worked at the Pub, cooking and delivering pizzas. I called Bill "Billy Boy" and he'd smile and say, "What you call me?"

And then J and I graduated from college, and we quit working at the Pub, because that's the kind of thing you stop doing when you're no longer in college. J went to graduate school in Portland because he and his brothers had all been born in Oregon before their dad got his job at the Naval Air Station in Nevada's desert, and that's why J loved the Seattle Mariners and the Supersonics too. J's reverence for Ken Griffey Jr. knew no bounds. He'd clenched his fists over the '98 season, as the Mariners slid in at third place in the AL West, back when Edgar Martinez and Alex Rodriguez swung bats for the M's, and Randy Johnson, ugly as sin, slung heaters from the mound. But the Mariners finished eleven games out. Still, better than my shitty Oakland A's who fell in last place. And J loved the big conifers of the Pacific Northwest, and he'd grown up in the 1990s, and his bedrooms were decorated with posters of Kurt Cobain and Layne Staley.

We always held parties at my family's cabin in Squaw Valley, near Lake Tahoe, and even after J moved to Portland he'd fly home and meet up with us and we'd all drive up there in the snow and sit around the fire or at the kitchen table drinking beer. Once my buddy Randy from back home in Monterey was up there with us, too, and he couldn't get over J, how he sat in front of the CD player replaying Alice in Chains's *Dirt* over and over, rocking his head as beer after beer disappeared down his throat. J would look at Randy and say, "Right here," pointing at the stereo, "This guitar right here," when a thundering chord landed, and he'd bow his head in reverence. Randy said, "I've never heard so much Alice in Chains in my life."

Once, J left a textbook he was teaching to his composition students up in Portland at the cabin and I found it but never returned it to him: *The Shape of Ideas* by Garrett Bauman. J was taking pedagogy courses for his Master's, and J had a sample assignment from some other composition professor, an assignment that presumably J was learning from so that he might learn how to give assignments, and this assignment sheet was folded in half and stuck in the middle of this book. The assignment sheet was for #3, due 10/25/95. In it the professor talks about quilts that have been handed down from his great-great-grandmother to his grandmother, to his mother, and finally to him, because he came from a family of all men, and now this nameless professor is learning to quilt. I meant to mail the book and assignment back to J, because I assumed he needed them, but he never called to ask about it, and I never got around to mailing it. I still have the book, and the assignment sheet is still folded and tucked in at the page number where J left it. I'm sentimental about such things. And now that's kind of how I see J: as that book, as if he himself is the book, that J is the shape of ideas. I like to think of the words in the assignment as belonging to J, even though I know that they're not. I like to think of J learning to quilt his history into permanence.

At his funeral the music matched his decade, except for the Beatles, which were his favorite band. First "Penny Lane" came on, then Temple of the Dog's "Say Hello to Heaven."

Funny, it wasn't what you'd think: no drugs, no fight, no bartime mishap. No jealous lover stabbed him in his back. J came into town to visit from Portland and he and Billy Boy went out, had some beers, stopped by the Pub and saw our friends, went to Jake and Shawna's house for dinner, and when they left Jake said they were fine, that they'd chilled without drinking for a long time before the drive back to Winnemucca. It was a pair of headlights that came out of the dark in the middle of the desert, on an expanse of U.S. Highway that's so straight it could be a massive ruler. These teenagers were out joyriding, their car's stereo blasting. On this road you can hit more than 150 mph if your car can reach it. These teens were passing a semi and so came into the lane of oncoming traffic. In the wreckage the police would find whisky and methamphetamine. They say J died instantly and painlessly. Bill was driving.

They say Bill's blood alcohol content was over the legal limit. They say the teen driver of the other car was the Sheriff's daughter. I hear that those three kids all lived. So did Bill.

At J's funeral Tiffany tried to talk and almost couldn't, she was crying too hard. She and J had been broken up already for over a year, since he'd left for Portland. I was living in Atlanta when Bob called to tell me, and Bob, even, was crying—a man who gutted deer, who popped off bunnies as if life had never existed and never mattered—so I cried, too. I came home, and I stepped to the microphone, and I recounted the last conversation J and I had had, just two weeks earlier:

Me: What are you doing?

J: Weeeeelllll, I waaaaaassssss on my way to work. Buuuuuuuut, now I'm talking to you and opening a beeeeeer.

Everyone laughed, and cried. I saw J and Bill's dad, and their mother, and Tom and his girlfriend, and Jake and Shawna and Mike and Chris and Timmy and Bob and Jasmine and Karen and Derrick and Cara and Larry and everyone—almost all of my friends from Reno because J had directly or indirectly introduced me to all of them and I said so. I told the crowd how I owed J for everything and everyone I knew and I think that that was true and still is.

Bill was not there. He sat at his parents' house with his broken leg and broken heart, and when I saw him at the wake he sobbed into my arms. After he cried he smiled. Then he broke down again. I thought of the Oakland A's and New York Yankees game that Billy Boy and I had attended a few years earlier, the postseason, and how Billy Boy had smiled the whole time and talked to my dad about the game. Now he had two months to heal before his arraignment, and today he's still in prison somewhere in Nevada.

I'm sure some people will think that my writing this is insensitive to the Joyner family. It's true that this ruined them. With J dead and Bill in prison, their parents divorced, as is often the case in families that face such devastating tragedy. Tom and his girlfriend had a baby and I think eventually married, but I have not spoken to them in almost ten years and I have no idea what's happened to them or their daughter though I hope they are all alive and healthy and happy. But I'm not writing this to tell you a sad story, or to instruct you on the risks of drinking and driving. I don't want to hurt my friends the Joyners any more than they've been hurt already. I just miss my friend, my friend whom I think if he'd lived might be writing himself, for he was a writer and a lover of literature. I just wish so much that he was alive and Bill were here, too, and not in jail where I haven't seen him. I wish we were listening to Alice in Chains. At least it's baseball season.

Never Pay for a Cab this Way if You Can Help It

I was in this fucked relationship with a woman who had the beginnings of a serious drinking problem. To be fair, I too swilled ten to twelve too many beers a day and was a heavy drug user. This girl and I had first kissed when she came to my apartment to smoke some pot and, at the time, she already had a boyfriend, so technically I "stole" her away, to use the ex-boyfriend's language, a man who told me this over yet more beers. Smoking pot, I know, is hardly "heavy drug use," but I didn't tell her about the cocaine and morphine and acid and magic mushrooms.

Within a couple months we moved into this tiny house down the street from the bar where we both worked. It was about two weeks in when we had our first serious fight and I shattered a table lamp against a wall. It would not be until much later that things got even worse (and that's a whole other story altogether), but let me sum this up by telling you that the story I want to tell is about the second time I tried to kill myself.

Both times I took a bunch of pills—painkillers—whole bottles' worth. The first time my girlfriend shoved her finger down my throat while I sat naked in the bathtub, and I puked out all these half-digested tablets that floated in a white froth that circled down the drain like a miniature galaxy being eaten by its own supermassive black hole. The second time, though, I was alone and puking wouldn't work, and after I realized that I didn't want to die (mostly because—as it is with all people who attempt suicide and fail—I was too much of a pussy to follow through) I called 911.

The cops drove me to the hospital themselves rather than calling an ambulance. I was starting to nod out, so I guess they figured they didn't have time to wait. When I woke up in the hospital, my throat hurt from the tubes they'd shoved down it to pump my stomach. The light was piercing, and a nurse shoved aside the curtain that walled me off and handed me a cup and said, "Drink this." It was liquid charcoal and it tasted exactly how you might think liquid charcoal would taste. I tried not to put my teeth together but when I did little bits of charcoal ground between them like I had a mouth full of silt. The drip line from a bag of fluid ran from the pole that held it into the needle that was in my arm.

When the doctor showed up he didn't say anything till after he'd looked in my eyes, then he asked how I felt, which was, other than a little grogginess and the aforementioned throat pain, fine. Then the doctor looked at me steadily and said, "Your girlfriend's here. Do you want to see her?"

It took me a minute. She was the reason I was in that emergency room in the first place. I guess *I* was the reason, but I can't remember what we were fighting about, and it doesn't matter anymore. What matters is that there I lay, and I said yes, and a minute or two later the curtain again swept aside and in walked my girlfriend.

I can tell you that she was a pretty girl in a kind of destroyed way. Her auburn hair was naturally curly and she'd sometimes go for days without brushing it, always rolling it up in a bun, and the tendrils would dread together. Her eyes were green, the lids heavy, so that until she got closer you might think that she was squinting at you. Her lips held a native pout. I was glad to see her, but all she said was, "You're not going home from here, you know that."

She said, "They're taking you down by the river."

The State Psychiatric Hospital was on the Truckee, and I knew that that was what my girlfriend meant, and I knew that I did not want to go there. Everything around me was turquoise: the curtain that walled me off, the lone chair covered with what looked like my clothes in the corner. The bed and its sheets were white. My gown, I would find out, was also turquoise but I didn't know that yet. After my girlfriend dispatched this info she kissed her fingertips and pressed them to my forehead and that was that.

The rest of this story is one of those you-won't-believe-this-because-this-could-only-happen-in-real-life-kind of stories.

Looking back, I don't know if what my girlfriend told me was true. I think there are some consent issues there, but maybe not. I *was* suicidal, even if I was too weak to pull it off, which I suppose made me even more of a danger to myself than someone more committed, because

I'd end up hurting my body pretty badly in all my failed attempts. But this is what happened: I listened to the sounds of the nurses and whoever else might be in that emergency room beyond the curtain, and when I thought they were on the room's opposite end or gone altogether I pulled the IV from my arm and sat up. I don't remember if this hurt, but there was blood.

On the chair I found my shirt and pants, but my shoes were not there, nor my keys or wallet. I didn't care. I slipped out of the hospital gown and into my clothes and, barefoot, I slinked out from behind that curtain and found my way to the waiting room and the world outside.

Fortunately, it was summer, as winters in Reno are pretty damn cold, like high desert cold, in the shadow of the Sierra Nevada Mountains and all their ski resorts looming to the west. But summer nights are warm, and the asphalt crinked up against the soles of my feet and I walked gingerly from the emergency room breezeway to the much smoother concrete sidewalk on Mill Street.

If you've ever been to Reno then you know that the Truckee Meadows consists of both Reno and Sparks—two cities that butt up against each other and make for one metro area. Each has its downtown made up of casino neon. Mill Street can take you from one casino district to the other, and in the flat expanse that makes up the valley in which these two cities sit—and with the confusion of nighttime and probably my head not clear from all the codeine they hadn't pumped from me—I started walking towards downtown Sparks and not Reno, where me and my girlfriend's little house lived.

And here, finally, I'm getting to the cab part. I don't know how far I walked before I realized I was going the wrong direction, but once I knew I decided I would not walk all the way back to Reno. When the cab passed and I hailed him he stopped. I said, "942 Ralston." The cab driver either did not see the blood congealing on my arm from where I'd pulled the IV free, nor my bare feet, or he decided that he'd seen weirder things.

In front of our house I told the cabbie to wait because the money was inside and I'd be right back. My girlfriend sat on the floor in front of the television. She looked at me the way someone looks at a ghost. I said, "I need seventeen dollars." But she didn't have any money. She would tell me stories of how, when she was a little girl, her mother got a job at Taco Bell so she could buy her daughters new school clothes because my girlfriend's father was too much of a cheapskate to pay for them. He once paddled my girlfriend because she sat in the shade of the cherry tree on a one-hundred-degree Los Angeles afternoon, and he caught her there, cooling off, when she was supposed to be raking the fallen cherries. She told me that she was eight years old when that happened. I loved this woman. It was a bad, desperate, mixed-up kind of love, but I loved her.

And here's the thing about codependent relationships: earlier that night, when we were both drunk and screaming at each other, we'd said the worst possible things humans who know each other intimately can say. And when I barged into our house after the cab dropped me off I didn't say hello, I didn't say I love you, I said "I need seventeen dollars." And my girlfriend who did not have the cash and who'd said the worst things to me—that I was fat and worthless, and no one would ever care about me at all—upended the change jar and sat on the floor with me in the blue glow from the television set, her tangled hair glinting in this dim light while her head nodded with her counting, as we added the quarters, dimes, and nickels up to twelve bucks. Twelve bucks: as much as I would end up paying for that hospital visit, despite the bills. And that pittance steamed the cabbie, as he glared at the paper sack of coins from his driver's side window after he'd waited these last fifteen minutes. But he took the change and drove away. And I went back inside our little house, and I slept by my girlfriend's side that night.

One Way to Survive an Abusive Relationship

It was not—as one might use the cliché—a one-way street. I was the one who threw that lamp against the wall where it shattered and the sparks sifted like fireworks falling in a heated sky till they faded and disappeared. My friend from school had left a message on our answering machine, inviting me to her birthday party. My girlfriend insisted that I had fucked this friend, that I was still fucking her. Why else would she invite *me* to the party, and *not explicitly also invite* my girlfriend? I was running around, I couldn't keep my dick in my pants, she should have known I was that kind of guy, why does she always do this, getting herself involved with people like me? My girlfriend wouldn't let me say anything. In frustration, I threw the lamp.

Her name was Karen and, looking back, I did truly love her. I was twenty-one years old, and Karen was twenty-eight. I hadn't had many girlfriends. There were a couple in high school, a few dates here and there, and a girl from Panama who hooked up with me during my sophomore year of college, but after summer came and went and she returned from vacation in New York, she wanted nothing to do with me and left me heartbroken, passed out in an easy chair with a half-emptied half gallon of Jack Daniels resting in my crotch. Karen told me that she'd already earned a BS in geology, that she was in the Master's program, that she was taking a break from school to work and live life. She was pretty, with slanting and slate-green eyes and auburn hair, pouting lips, an athlete's physique. She was a rock climber. For most of our relationship I worried that I'd never again in life have anyone who seemed as great as Karen, so I thought I'd better hold on to her.

That's what happens in your twenties. It's the last turn in the last lap that is the NASCAR race of your youth. I *could* have married Karen. I'm lucky I never got her pregnant. Only in retrospect can I see how either scenario might have been, and how these would have equaled the massive multi-car pileup and explosion and burned limbs that would accompany the analogy I've used above to illustrate this period in my life. Karen and I dated for four years. When it ended for good I was only four years away from meeting my wife, after I got out of the mess my relationship with Karen had made of my life. But Karen and I easily—all too easily—could have ruined the rest of our lives. As it is, I made that last turn. I nudged a few bumpers along the way to the finish line, but I cruised out of my twenties relatively unscathed. Race over.

What I've learned is that Karen and I were not codependent, as so many people over the years sounded so confident in calling us, and I used to think that we were codependent until I actually did some reading on the matter. I didn't seek affirmation from Karen, nor did she look for approval from me, and neither of us cared for the other excessively in a way that we neglected our own needs; we were equally self-destructive. What we did have were budding drug and alcohol problems and that, combined with a natural bit of chemical imbalance, created the mayhem in which I lived for those four years.

I should've seen the warning signs when we started dating. She had a boyfriend. I even set them up. He was my friend's friend, my friend from poetry workshop at school. We sat at a table on the Pub's front porch in early summer, the night warm enough in the high desert for short sleeves and cold pitchers. Karen said, "Who's the guy you're sitting with?"

Karen told me that when I started at the Pub (she trained me) she took me seriously when she asked what I wanted to do in life and I said, "Become a professional wrestler." My head was shaved at the time, and I'm pretty big and wore a goatee, so I could see how she might've taken this literally, though I was trying to be funny. Who knows what happened? I can rub off on people. I start to look not-so-bad over time, if you get to know me. One night after closing the Pub, Karen asked if I had any weed, which I did, at my apartment in the alley.

When we kissed I was upside down. I mean, I was lying on my couch, and Karen sat in the adjacent armchair and she leaned over me so that, when our mouths met, my nose touched her chin. We were stoned, and a little beer buzzed, and Karen knew it wasn't right and she got up to leave, saying that she had a boyfriend after all. I offered to walk her the block and a half to her house. When we got there, her boyfriend was waiting at the curb in his '57 Chevy (he was one of *those* guys, which I feel comfortable saying, since he and I—believe it or not—are still friends).

For the next couple months Karen and I would sneak makeout sessions in the hall between the employee entrance and the Pub's kitchen, or upstairs in the dough room, or in the walk-ins. I pestered her about breaking up with her boyfriend, but Karen persisted, saying she loved him. I should've known that the situation was bad then. How could I bring myself to hurt this couple by interfering? My self-esteem was so low that I went for pussy wherever I could get it, and—though I wasn't getting it at all—I had a girl kissing me, which meant the promise of more. Or so I thought. Add to this disastrous recipe the fact that Karen continued making out with me when she claimed to love her boyfriend, and the whole thing was made for disaster. Maybe not. It's the kind of thing you do in your twenties.

I was the drug *and* alcohol problem and Karen had booze cravings—real booze cravings, like beer-in-the-morning cravings. Karen smoked some weed, like I did, but she told me—explicitly—that she would never date a cokehead. So I didn't tell her about the crack period I'd already gone through, or the occasional gram that ended up in my pocket and that disappeared within a few hours. I never told her about the little blue bag containing the yellow rock of tweek that Rich, who worked in the kitchen, found on the street one day, and how I smoked the whole thing in one bowl, then puked all over Rich's bathroom. In fact, while we were dating it's safe to assume that my drug intake actually went down quite a bit.

It was not long after Karen broke up with her boyfriend that she asked me to move in with her. She suggested it and I saw no reason not to. I'd never lived with a woman before. In fact, not counting the college dorms, I'd only ever had one roommate. I don't remember discussing the idea with my parents. I was month-to-month with my landlord and I simply said that at the end of (fill in month here because god knows what month it was—didn't I tell you I had substance abuse problems?—but I think it was in the winter because I remember a day with snow) I'd be moving out. I already drove a truck, and I was literally moving a block and a half away. No problem. Then we were together in her little house peacefully for one month before I threw that lamp.

Karen was unreasonably jealous. When college girls came into the Pub in their summer short shorts she'd cry, look down and say, "I can't compete." She'd say, "Listen, I know you want to fuck those girls, so don't hide it." This came from my girlfriend with the six-pack abs. I tried to assuage her fears, to convince her that I loved her and was true to her. But then we got drunk.

Once we got into a fight while camping in Dog Valley, in the Sierra Nevada Mountains, twenty miles on dirt roads from Reno. Karen walked along beside the truck, screaming how much she hated my fat fucking guts. I said, "Just get in the car." After twenty minutes I threatened to leave. When she kept hollering, I followed through with that threat. I drove back to Reno. I met my friends and got drunk. I don't know who she thumbed a ride from once she reached I-80.

I packed up my things and moved out no fewer than three times within the space of about six months. I lived at my family's cabin in Squaw Valley, and once moved back in with my parents in California for a month. When Karen drove to my parents' house looking for me, and after we talked things out over a beer at the Castroville Inn where a Mexican lady stared at me and smiled her toothless smile, I packed up and moved back. That afternoon, my dad told me that the pretty blonde graduate student who was renting a room from our next door neighbor stopped by to see if I wanted to get a beer the very afternoon that I moved back to Reno, and that might've been bullshit because my dad was scared, not knowing when he'd get a call from the Reno PD that my throat had been slit, but he kept all of this from me until everything was done and I lived in Georgia and he knew that I was safe.

Our fights got so bad that Karen grabbed my suits out of the closet and, bare-handed, ripped them to shreds. All of my guitars splintered, smashed against walls, smashed against the concrete of the sidewalk, tossed into Ralston Street's sad traffic. I took a butcher knife to Karen's gowns, one an Oleg Casini, beaded and beautiful. And Karen had looked beautiful in it, too, that night before Christmas when we danced to jazz in that restaurant at Lake Tahoe. I took the knife to her blouses and sweaters, some that had been her grandmother's, fabric Karen cherished. Karen punched me in the face, blackened my eyes, bloodied and swelled my lips. I never touched her in a violent way, but I took it out on her possessions. A thirty-six-inch television sputtered and sparked in the corner where I threw it, and I had to put out the fire it started. The cops knew us by first name. A neighbor stopped me, blood dripping from my face, and I saw the fear and disbelief in this neighbor's eyes as she hollered at me to get a hold of myself.

We kept going back to each other because we were addicted. Neither one of us was the glutton for punishment, nor the oppressor who lavished control. We were equally, like the substances that fueled these fights, coursing through each other's veins, making us elated and enthralled with love one morning, and stomping down the street in our underwear that night, shamefaced and drunk, downing whole bottles of painkillers, having hospitals pump our stomachs.

To get out, I moved away. This happened in stages. Finally, everything crashed around me, not long after that night I tried walking home from the hospital after ripping the IV from my arm, and trudging a mile and a half in the wrong direction in bare feet down Mill Street, going from Reno into Sparks. I knew that I had to get out of the house that Karen and I shared. My old landlord set me up in an apartment with a balcony that overlooked the Truckee River. Karen moved to Los Angeles, where she was from, for six months. Her mother came to town and helped her to pack what was left of her things.

I'll never forget the look on Karen's mom's face when I stopped by as they wrapped dinner plates in newspaper and packed them into boxes and I stood outside the yard's gate with a solitary rose pinched between my fingers. I don't recall anyone, ever or since, wearing such hatred when she stared at me. The drop in my gut when, after a few empty phone calls, Karen's voice peeped through on the other end, all the way from LA, tentative, sad: "Jamie?" Within a couple of weeks I was in my truck headed south on I-395 past the eastern scarp of the Sierra Nevada Mountains and through the desert, a pilgrim to my destructive love.

I remembered the last time we'd driven 395 together, on the way to Karen's sister's wedding. We thought we'd make a trip out of it and camp along the way. But our fights. We stopped in one windy, ravine oasis, and after hollering at each other, and after Karen got into the car and began to drive away, I had the knife in my hand, and the insanity rollicking through me made it so that I hadn't any choice: I stabbed the tire. We were in the fucking desert. I kicked sand and dust into Karen's head while she cussed me and attempted to lug on the spare. When we got to LA, and Karen threw a cheeseburger in my face and then nearly ran me over (and literally did run over my foot as I tried to jump out of the way), and I put my fist through the driver's side window and sent pieces of glass like a million diamonds raining over Karen's face and the truck's interior, I knew that In-n-Out Burger would never be the same for me again. The employees at the hotel I walked to wouldn't give me a room, though their sign read "Vacancy," and the couple in line in front of me had just sauntered off, room key in hand, looking back warily at the lettuce and secret sauce in my hair as I bled on the lobby tiles.

Eventually Karen returned to Reno, to her own apartment, and I inhabited mine. And we maintained a rocky, on again, off again—but not nearly so tempestuous—relationship for the next three years. I lied to my family: Sure I saw Karen at the Pub and around town, but we weren't dating. I wasn't crazy. When my sister visited, and Karen stopped by our barstools for a nervous hello, it was all my sister could do not to throttle Karen right then. But I bullshitted Meghann: "Don't worry. We're just friends now."

I was lucky that, over these years, whatever burned inside me when I met Karen fizzled, and I got more serious about writing. And when I was accepted into a graduate creative writing program across the country, I did not hesitate to agree to the accompanying teaching offer. It was time to move on. Reno, Nevada held nothing more for me in terms of my becoming a writer, and by this time my desire to be a writer had consumed my desire for Karen. So, leaving town and leaving Karen was a no-brainer. I *had* to go. Before I left Reno, pulling along my U-haul full of shit that had not been destroyed while Karen and I dated, I stopped by the Pub to say goodbye to some folks and Karen was not amongst them, and I didn't care.

Even when I made it to Atlanta, and settled into my first apartment, in a past where Americans maintained land lines and listed phone numbers in a database called the "White Pages," I answered the ringing to that same sad and tentative voice crying out from 2,500 miles away. Only then was I scared. Only then did I cut off such telephones and live a cellular life.

I've returned many times to Reno to visit my friends, or give readings at the independent bookstore and at my alma mater, and I've seen Karen. She looks the same, with a little gray at her temples. One time she hugged me, the only time in ten years that we've touched. I've since quit smoking, and the reek of cigarettes clinging to her jacket and hair was not Karen's smell that I remembered. It was not the aroma left on her bandana, the one I found in my apartment as I packed to leave Reno, and that I kept with me in a bag socked away in a closet for too long a time. My friends, even, have grown older and more sober. Their children are in schools and lunches must get made and clothing bought, medical insurance provided for. No one hangs out at the Pub anymore.

And me: my first years in Atlanta were depressed coke-and-booze-fueled romps drawn out in an attempt to alleviate the loneliness of having left the friends and town I'd known since I was eighteen. But all that partying got old—boring even—and I knew that it wasn't healthy, and it was doing nothing for my sex life. I decided to get my shit together. I quit doing drugs and cut back on drinking. I wanted to meet someone with whom I could maintain a relationship, and I knew that that wasn't going to happen by meeting a girl in a bar while I was geetered out on cocaine. I focused on the doctorate degree that had brought me to Atlanta. I dove into reading and writing. Eventually, I joined eHarmony, and there I met the woman who would become my wife. And once I knew I was falling in love with her, I knew that I'd never snort another line of cocaine, that I'd never suck on another Camel. But it's safe to assume that I won't forget what I came from. Obviously, since you're reading this, I'm still trying to put out the light that shines on this part of my past. But I don't think I have the strength to shatter it against a bare wall. Maybe it's better that it shines, if dimly, a light in a receding tunnel, and I'm on my way out the other end.

13 Steps to Becoming a Barslut, and What Happens Afterwards

After I moved across the country from the town where I'd spent my college years, where I'd acquired a network of friends, in my new city I was lonely and depressed. I found a bar down the street from my new apartment, a metal bar—as in a bar where metalheads hung out and Ozzy played, either with Sabbath or not, continuously over the speakers. There I ate bacon cheeseburgers and drank no fewer than thirteen PBRs a night. I became what they call a regular and the other regulars and the bartenders pushed Jäger and Strega shots my way. I bought grams of coke and keyed it in the bathroom stall. One night I got so drunk and high that when I passed out at home I slept for two days and woke at sundown, thinking only the day after that night had passed and I went right back to that bar and got messed up again and only learned about my missed day when I saw the date on the bar's television.

I gained thirty pounds, pushing my way to 270. And worst of all: I got no pussy.

After an Xmas photo revealed to me the extent of my double chin I decided that this no pussy-getting-depressed-lifestyle sucked. I cut out drinking except for one night a week. I hardly ate anything at all. I still walked to the train to get to work and the sweat dripped off me and so too dripped the weight. I was a melting candle.

Every day, especially when coming home from work, I walked past the sports bar (a different bar than the metal bar down the street, but I frequented this place, too) and I could feel the tug of the beer and chicken wings in my mouth, down my throat, but I pushed on.

I slept a lot.

On that single Friday night when I allowed myself to drink, I also allotted whatever food I wanted. But my stomach had shrunk. I'd order a pizza and pop a Netflix movie into my computer and after a slice I sat there feeling like I'd eaten another human while Val Kilmer went to Mars. I would also pick up a six-pack of Sam Adams, and I'd nurse a solitary beer until midnight.

Then, after midnight, like some lame Clapton song, I went to the bar: that metalhead bar that on weekends filled with more than metalheads, and there I trolled for strange.

I had a system worked out:

> **1**: Arrive at bar sober and after midnight (as described above).

2: Stand—do not sit—at bar and nurse PBR.

3: Wait for drunk girls to come to bar to pay their tabs.

4: Attempt casual conversation w/out caring if they reciprocate.

5: When they do: bonus.

6: Keep cocaine use to minimum (see, "effects of cocaine" below).

7: Ask the girls who start a conversation many questions. Act (and sometimes genuinely feel) very interested in them.

8: When, after ~twenty mins of chitchat, girl puts bar receipt into purse and says, "It was nice talking to you, but I should get going," look surprised at bartenders shoving glasses into dishwasher as they ready to close and agree that you also must be getting home.

9: Just before girl walks away, say, "Hey, would you mind if I got a ride? I live just up the street." This, of course, turns out to be true.

10. If girl says sorry but no, smile, say, "No problem, it was good talking to you." If girl shrugs, says sure, bonus, but not there yet.

11. In girl's car, instruct her up the street half block to outside of apartment building where, conveniently, there's no shoulder or parking space to pull into. Instruct girl to drive around block to your off-street parking. This, you remind her, is for her own safety.

12. Upon dropoff say: "I've got a couple drinks in the house, if you'd like one."

13. If girl says no thanks, see 10 above. If girl says yes: cha-ching. Done.

By this method of restrictive diet plus calculated luring of women into one-night stands, in a period of six months I bedded nine women, thus destroying my depression, and boosting my self-confidence.

I wanted to be a slut. I rarely had sex with the same girl more than once. Sometimes I'd run into former hookups at the same or another bar. Only once did a former hookup give me that *you motherfucker* look and approached while I was picking up yet another woman to say, "So, who's this?" (introducing herself to the new girl), and after a few awkward moments of the former hookup trying to make it obvious to the new girl that I had banged her and never called her afterwards (and she made this perfectly obvious by saying, "You never called me. What the hell?"), she walked away, and the new girl didn't seem to care at all. In fact, I think that might have made me even more desirable. I guess I looked like someone whom other women found desirable? Maybe some girls are into jerks?

Effects of cocaine: cocaine did not help my dick to work at all. I've had friends who said that when they got hard and they were all geetered out, their boner never went away and they weren't going to sleep, so it was just screw all night long. Not me. So I learned to curb the coke if I wanted to get laid.

This period of my life was all *me* time. I was selfish, and that contributed to the randomness of these hookups.

So what happened? What happens when you're a barslut? It eventually gets really, really old. Usually, the sex was pretty mechanical. I treated each woman kindly and respectfully. I did not have the audacity to pull off some porno-like ass-smacking or money shots. For one thing, in a hookup I was vulnerable. I didn't want to reveal too much of myself for fear of turning a woman off or scaring her, so I played things fairly safe. But I did get better at sex.

I wanted to know what might happen if in these hookups I devoted myself to the woman's pleasure. I tried hard to make every girl I took home come, and come hard. The result was that girls blew up my cell and showed up unannounced at my apartment. One girl followed me in her car for thirty miles when I drove to a friend's place north of the city. When we stopped, in front of this friend's driveway, she said, "I just really wanted to see you."

But what ultimately happened was that I met a girl I liked. Not only would she not allow us to have sex after a first date, then a second, and a third—not for about two weeks—but when we finally did and she came, I knew I wanted to make her come again, and again, and I still love it when she comes now that we're married, because it feels good to make her feel good, because she is sweet, and she believes in me, because back then she was going to become a lawyer, and now she is one, and she saw that I was much more than the slut I'd made myself out to be, and I liked the way her brown hair dropped over her little ears, and I still like her hair and her ears, and we keep at it, and I don't do coke anymore.

The Most Disgusting Things I Did While I Was a Smoker

If you've read this far you know that I have—ahem—a *history* with substance abuse. Of all these drugs that I did and quit using, the hardest of all to quit was smoking cigarettes. For that reason, if you're a smoker, some of the things I list here will maybe not seem that disgusting. However, once you quit, if you do quit, you'll see just how gross these behaviors are.

1. Simply smoking. And smoking and smoking and smoking. Usually, as a result of inebriation I would chain smoke. Packs disappeared. I kept buying, and I kept smoking. After a few days of that, when I'd come off a bender, the tips of my index and middle fingers and my thumb on

my left hand were tinted yellow (also, not necessarily smoking related, I don't think, but when you're all messed up like this it's impossible to keep your fingernails clean, so there was always a scrim of black underneath them), and my hair reeked. I always thought it was the drugs and/or alcohol that made me smoke like that. But I've known people who chain smoke and who hardly ever touch a drop of booze. That's how grossly powerful nicotine is.

2. Smoking a cigarette first thing in the morning. There's nothing like waking up after a night out at the bar with your buddies, or fighting with your bipolar girlfriend till the point that you say *fuck it* and ditch her and buy that day's second pack of cigarettes after the gram of coke you also purchased in your giving up on life, and after smoking all but three smokes in that pack, and you find the first of those three and light up. Your lungs are already wheezing. You cough, hock a brownish loogie flecked with black, sometimes with blood. You haven't brushed your teeth in a few days. That's one fine cigarette.

3. The airport smoking lounge. This is a dank and depressing hovel set away from normal people and filled with reeking rows of airport seating covered with pleather that has cured in the nicotine-drenched carbon monoxide atmosphere. There are air conditioners and "smoke eaters" running, but they do no good for the number of smokers huddled in this tiny room. If there are plants in this room to "cheer the joint up,"

the plants are dead or dying. Through the haze of smoke one might try to make out the images on the television that floats somewhere overhead. The worst thing to see in a smoking lounge is families: mothers and fathers shushing their kids while said kids attempt desperately to entertain themselves in this toxic environment while mom and dad get their nic fix. You can imagine what these parents might look like; they look exactly what you'd think parents who take their kids into the smoking lounge look like: there's a lot of tank tops and/or muscle shirts and jean cutoffs and tattoos of Calvin pissing, or of Yosemite Sam flaunting his pistols complete with the "Stay Back!" epitaph. Both these kinds of tattoos can also be found as stickers on these parents' vehicles. Here I am describing this with chagrin while there I sat, smoking my own cigarettes, in the haze that was my drug-addled brain, and usually these parents would start talking to me and, at the time, I'd think they were pretty cool in the end. The second worse thing to see is old people, some of them carting oxygen tanks in those wheeled carts, and sucking their cigarettes while the tubes run from the tank to their nose. I'd watch these poor souls and hope that I wouldn't ever be one of them while I smoked myself into not caring about my inability to drum up the willpower to try to keep myself alive.

4. Sharing cigarettes with strangers. I'm at the bus stop one day, and I've run out of smokes, and I've got a thirty-minute ride to work, which hap-

pens to be in an area where I'll need to walk a half mile to the gas station where I can buy a new pack. But there's a young woman, in fact from this distance she doesn't appear to be too bad looking, and she's smoking a cigarette. So I approach, ask if I can bum one. Alas, it's her last. But she cordially offers to share this last and already lit cigarette with me. Before I go on, let me explain that I am maybe recently awakened from some night sucking down Jägermeister till I did some fancy walking, and I'm not quite the fresh face myself. But it's only when I sit next to this woman on the bus station bench and she passes me the cigarette, the butt a little moist from her lips or her tongue or both, and as I'm taking a few drags I see her teeth, many of which are missing or in a state of decay. She's also one of those people whom you realize that when they talk, gobs of spit and mucus crowd up in the corners where her lips meet. She's got a severe overbite. She proceeds to tell me that she's waiting for the bus that will take her to a job interview, her first in eighteen months. She just got out of jail.

5. Sharing cigarettes with friends. All of the above details are almost exactly the same with the exception of having already been well acquainted with the person with whom I was smoking.

6. Roll yr own. I don't mean with Bugler, or Bali Shag. I mean that it's three AM and I've run out of cigarettes, but I'm still a little drunk, or maybe tripping or gacked or something, but I've got

ashtrays full of butts and, lucky for me, I'm a drug user, so rolling papers are always within reach. Some jackass once told me that it was good for my plants if I put my butts into the soil, and I want a cigarette bad enough to retrieve even these molding spent cigs, turning some shade between green and blue. I crack all these open into a heap of stinking, mostly burnt tobacco that I roll into new cigarettes. This tastes exactly how you imagine it might taste. It tastes like shit, if shit tasted like previously smoked, multi-day-and-in-some-cases-multi-week-and-month-old cigarette tobacco. But I don't care; I've got my smoke now and afterward I can pass out and later wake and, without showering or brushing my teeth, walk to the Texaco for a fresh pack.

7. Smoking butts found on the ground or in public ashtrays. At least I had smoked most of the butts I found in the ashtrays and in my planters around my apartment. But there were too many times when I found myself down to my last ten dollars and I did what any sensible alcoholic would do with that money: I went to the bar. At the bar where I kicked it, PBRs were a dollar, so that meant ten beers (sorry, no tip). And what to do for smokes? I bummed some, but when that had run its course I reverted to scavenging the bar ashtrays. Sometimes I'd take that little bit of money to the convenience store for forties, and then, while drinking and walking back to my apartment, I scoured the sidewalks for butts that had at least a centimeter of un-

smoked tobacco remaining. Anything more than a centimeter was a significant score. I remember my buddy Mike once exclaiming upon a merely half-smoked sidewalk cigarette, "Hell yeah!" and we shared that. So combine this layer of gross with layer 5 above.

8. Drying out wet cigarettes. I've done this, yes: jumped into the lake and, whoops, cigs still in pocket (along with wallet, lighter, keys, etc.). I'm that kind of idiot. I'm also the kind of idiot who's like, *I ain't letting this full pack of smokes go to waste*. So I set them in the sun, dried them out, and smoked them. They tasted like algae.

9. Accidentally drinking from a beer-turned-ashtray. I think people have depicted this happening in movies. I'm not sure about that though. But I've done it. What's worse is not realizing that's what's happened until a few drinks in. What happens is you pick up a beer you think is yours, or the party's ended and there aren't any beers left, but you just really need one and you hunt up half-drunk beers littering the coffee table or the kitchen counter. That first sip is just a little flat, or at least that's all you notice. Then you detect a strange, almost metallic flavor. By the time you take the sip that brings the cigarette butt(s) to the beer can's opening, where it comes up against your lips, maybe your teeth, and you finally realize what's going on, you've also realized that that flavor is of already-smoked-cigarette. I've thrown up because of this. I have also not thrown up and continued in my quest for part-drunk beers that did not become ashtrays.

10. Relapsing. I quit smoking and doing drugs because I got tired of the life, and I was lonely, and I knew that if I wanted to meet a girl of the marrying type I was unlikely to find her in the bar crowds that I ran with. I stopped going to bars so often. When I met my wife I was "smoke free." Those quotation marks are there because, like I said, I've never had so much trouble quitting anything like I had trouble quitting nicotine. Every once in a while—like at my brother's wedding, where I ran into some of my childhood friends who smoked—I'd bum a cigarette, smoke all or half of it, and disgust myself in the process.

I hate to sound all preachy, like, *I quit, and you're a loser for not seeing how gross that habit is*. What I mean is that I understand the pull that tobacco has on someone who's been using it for some time. And because I've felt that, I'm also able to see what stupid and gross things that pull made me do. I'm in no "higher" a place for having quit. I still feel cigarettes tugging at my will. I tend to stay out of places that allow smoking, because a few drinks in I start to crave them, and with the alcohol I feel my willpower crumbling away. I'm an immensely weak person. If I only think about the dumb and gross things I've done and could do again, maybe I'll make this not smoking thing stick.

What It's Really Like

You're sixteen and hanging out with your buddies at a friend's trailer because his dad's out of town and you decide you're gonna get fucked up, so you drink a six pack of beer in under a half hour. The last things you remember are sitting down to take a crap then your buddies laughing you awake when you pass out with your pants around your ankles. The next day, along with your hangover come stories about all the hilarity you caused during your blackout. How you spelled "Fuck You" with your piss on the driveway of some girl who dissed you. How you told the waitress at the diner downtown to go to hell when she told your friends to get your drunk ass out of there before she called the cops. Man, what fun times you laugh over! That's one way this whole thing starts, when you're a teenager, and you think that getting totally smashed is both fun and funny.

But it doesn't stay that way. Because the good times roll over into college. The parties blur together: nights stumbling home down the hills of a darkly lit desert city. Finding that your friends, in your drunken stupor, had taken markers to your face and drew cocks aimed at your mouth and scribbled epithets usually found on bathroom stall walls on your forehead. You have no idea how long they were there before you now see them in the mirror. Then the rest of your twenties roll by, where you've worked up to beers with sidecars, and remember that time you almost went to jail when you choked that racist up against the bar's wall for saying that he thought white people were superior to blacks? Sober, you'd have walked away, disgusted that someone said that, knowing you were smarter, and perhaps pitying the person who thought so small. But drunk, you fell to violence. And you find yourself in your thirties, and you obsess over some startling new symptoms.

You get emotional: angry, sentimental, happy, etcetera. These emotions emit via diatribes that don't make sense, like when I got upset at my family because—from my drunk perspective—they didn't care about the "state of world affairs" and were content to go on living their blissfully ignorant lives, la la la. Did I tell you that this occurred one year on Christmas night? I called my mom a bitch when she told me to shut up already. I threw up in my sister's kitchen sink. The next morning I apologized to everyone, but this kind of damage goes unrepaired, really.

Sometimes you endure extreme pain. You get muscle cramps. Alcohol dehydrates the drinker and interferes with the delivery of electrolytes to muscles. On top of this, you're a jogger, and you live in Atlanta, and muscle overexertion in hot weather contributes to these painful spasms. They usually manifest in the hamstrings and calves, and they almost always happen sometime in the middle of the night. It's like someone has tied a string around one end of a muscle without your knowing it, then they give it a yank and hold the string taught. It hurts like hell. The other night I had a severe cramp while sleeping in a tent (I was camping). The only way to end a cramp and the pain is to stretch it out or to leap up and get weight on my leg. Neither's very easy when you're wrapped in a sleeping bag on the ground in the woods. So I just lay there and grunted and screamed and there was nothing to be done but wait painfully for it to pass, which took five excruciating minutes.

You also get these strange muscular and nerve problems, like when you're sleeping you get the pins and needles in your hands and arms. Yeah, lots of people get this, but your case is different, because it happens pretty much every night. You've figured out ways to sleep that help to prevent this, like when sleeping on your stomach you tuck one hand under your head and the other under your chest/belly, and this alternating arm position seems to reduce the symptoms. But you have other issues. Ever have the strange, involuntary and sudden sensation that you're falling? You get this almost every night, out of nowhere, and it startles you awake, which can contribute to the insomnia (covered below).

Your blood pressure spikes, and if you're me you can actually feel it. It's like the blood pumping up my carotid artery and into my brain vibrates against my skull so I hear the pulses in my ears and they won't go away. You get night sweats. You have insomnia. You lie awake reading and writing. This is excellent for your productivity, but not so good for getting to work the next day after a sleepless night.

Night terrors: these aren't nightmares, as you don't achieve REM sleep. That's because, as previously mentioned, you cannot sleep. But you sometimes do get into a weird half-awake/half-asleep state in which you think you can see everything in the room in which you lie. The details are extraordinary. There's the television, the coffee table, the remote. You feel the fabric of the couch beneath you. But you cannot move. You're paralyzed. And what's more awful is that you hear the footsteps (someone's, but whose?) approaching from behind. Then you feel whoever that is touching your shoulder, pushing against you. You're so goddamn scared because you cannot see who or what this is because you cannot move to see the person or to make him stop, or to get away, or to fight back. Then your eyes snap open to the living room, empty except for you lying there. You return to your book, the lines of prose running by like marching armies. When you doze, repeat at this paragraph's beginning. The process continues till morning.

You retain water, even as you take in excessive amounts of water after exercising or when you drink beer. Add to this the fact that you spend an inordinate amount of time in bars and thus dine on bar foods loaded with salt that also contributes to water retention. All this water in all of your cells, including your red blood cells, causes the hypertension your doctor diagnoses you with and for which he prescribes Lisinopril, and tells you to cut out salts, change your diet, and lose weight. Once you even successfully followed the doctor's recommendations for almost a week prior to a doctor's appointment. At that appointment, when your doctor asked, and you truthfully (for that one-week period, at least) responded, he said, "That's not too bad." And with your confidence you explained that you only let loose on the weekend. That was when your doctor's eyebrows raised and he looked at you incredulously, saying, "Only on the *weekend*?" And you did not have the strength to explain that most of the time it's like last weekend times five.

Diarrhea. You'll rarely ever poop solid. Sorry, yes this is gross, but it's the truth. See, because your lower intestine is inflamed and this inhibits water reuptake via your bowels, so you'll poop watery stools regularly. Also, your pancreas is fucked up and inflamed. The enzymes the pancreas normally secretes in order to help digest food don't get where they need to go in the stomach, so all that nutrition you're supposed to get doesn't end up in your body as it passes in that watery stool, wasted, like your body, which is wasting away. The other thing that sucks about this is the diarrhea splatters that have to be cleaned off the underside of your toilet seat and in your toilet bowl, if you ever anticipate company. And it's not like you can just do this once a week or something. You pretty much have to clean up after every movement, the likes of which can sometimes top six a day because, well, you probably already know what having diarrhea's like. Imagine this being a 365-days-per-year kind of thing.

Another thing that sucks is trying to find time. Unfortunately, most people, myself included, are fairly responsible, have jobs and families, and work hard to maintain the personal and professional relationships that help perpetuate these scenarios. Because such work has to be put into such relationships, necessarily one loses time. But, if you're honest with yourself, you realize that a good portion of your thinking per day goes into how you will make time. You'll think things like, I've got just ten minutes, but if I use it then I won't get the emissions test done on the car, but I could get that done tomorrow. I mean, the registration's already expired, so what does one more day matter? You'll think: my wife leaves work at 5:30 PM, so if I've got time after I've finished teaching, I can make up some time, then go to the grocery store and go home to make dinner, then, after the wife goes to bed I'll have even more time then. For at least a little while every day you'll think about that story you're working on and the sentences that accompany it, and rarely you'll have great spurts during which you'll write insatiably. All this creates an air of efficiency and productivity.

The good news is that there are millions of people like you! Most people can't fess up to the facts. Your own family is this way: they can't admit that there's a history here on both your father's and your mother's sides, nor can they accept it when you tell them. They say, *You have a job! You're responsible!* However, you have at least accepted the truth and you're able to at look yourself. Hence the sleepless nights. Because I try so hard. I've learned to work my way through multiplication tables in order to get at least a little sleep. I poop solids! My health has returned and the doctor says I might go off the blood pressure meds. I tell myself the truth daily. I write essays about the truth about myself! I keep telling myself: This is evidence that you're more productive with your work. What's left to work on is watching your children grow into adults. And you're working in that direction. That's all you need to tell yourself. Tell yourself this every day: that you're working so goddamn hard.

A Brief, Depressing, Hilarious, Disgusting History with Pickup Lines

Any time I've ever tried to use a pickup line I was young and drunk. Today I'm happily married. As it is with my wife, any significant relationship I ever had with a woman came about rather organically, when I met people in benign situations (i.e., I wasn't trying to "get" with them), then I got to know those people better and, in some cases, romantic relationships ensued.

Seems that pickup lines are for when you *are* trying to "get" with someone. They're like the taglines an automobile manufacturer uses in its television commercials. They are the spirit of disingenuousness. But they do make for some sad/funny stories.

I just wanted to tell you that I think you're beautiful . . .

This is, depending on your point of view, a sad, or silly and juvenile story. But it might be funny, too. I'd gone to a Bob Dylan show as part of the Reno Hilton's outdoor summer concert series. I was in this I-should-probably-see-as-many-great-musicians-from-before-I-was-born-before-they're-all-dead phase. I saw acts like Buddy Guy, Eric Clapton, Etta James, The Grateful Dead, James Taylor, that sort of stuff. But what's important here is that I'd eaten an eighth of mushrooms and I peaked during this show. It really was magical, blah, blah. But, seriously, Reno is in the high desert, on the eastern side of the Sierra Nevada Mountains, so when storms come tumbling over those peaks, they usually dump off all their moisture on the western windward side, then dissipate over the desert (the rain shadow)—hence the desert being a desert. But sometimes the storms were too intense, and they didn't lose everything and so carried their strength into the valley of the Truckee Meadows. This happened the summer afternoon of this particular Bob Dylan concert when I was tripping out on psilocybin. The sun was going down, and so made a band of bright orange and slowly-dimming-to-purple light in the slit of sky on the horizon between the mountains and the storm clouds. From these clouds lightning flashed to the valley floor. The wind blew strong, but warm, a soft breath over my whole body. I stood at the pinnacle of the temporary bleachers the Hilton set up in the parking lot each year for this concert series. And there, among this atmospheric spectacle, and under the influence of these drugs, I met a petite brunette with the most dazzling green eyes I've ever seen. We talked for what seemed an hour. I was mesmerized. And the whole thing started because I had balls enough—or my inhibitions were down enough—that when I noticed her, I said the line above, which wasn't so much a line, but complete drug-addled honesty. And, at least, so I thought, we "hit it off." I remember that, after the concert, when she and her friends were leaving, and I and my friends, we parted with a hug, though I never got her phone number or anything because, I thought, it was just one of those magical things. But what's weird is that I did see her again, not two weeks later, at a Fourth of July party in Squaw Valley in Lake Tahoe. Again, we were listening to a band, this time some asshole's garage band playing off a cabin deck. And when I saw this girl and recognized her, I thought, *Holy shit, this has to mean something.* So I felt compelled to talk to her again. I walked up and leaned in for a hug hello, but she drew back, wary. I think she even said, "Whoa, dude, what are you doing?" She didn't remember me at all. When I reminded her of the Dylan show she claimed to remember, but the look on her face told me otherwise. She mumbled something about being "a little drunk that night." Ha. She went on to tell me about how she had the hots for the dumbass playing bass in the shitty bad punk band we were listening to, but mostly it seemed she just wanted me to go away. I did. I returned to my own cabin and got drunk because what matters? Nothing matters! The world is awful! I think I was twenty years old.

**What is that that
smells so good?
Ah, it's you ladies . . .**

I used to hang out at this bar in Midtown Atlanta that's no longer there, a place called Vickery's. My buddy—the poet Mike Dockins—and I were regulars there, and we'd sit at the bar for hours and get into ridiculous conversations/rants about the most mundane of things. Once we had an hours-long session talking about how air is dumb, because most people just say "air" or think that it's mostly oxygen, when in fact a larger portion of what we breathe as "air" is nitrogen, and there's the "trace elements." Oh how Dockins loves the trace elements. We always drank PBR, which they served on draft to restaurant industry employees for a dollar a pint. Neither of us worked at a restaurant; we were PhD. students. But they served us at the industry price anyway. So it was easy enough for me and Mike to get through quite a few beers without emptying our wallets of our meager graduate student stipends. It was actually cheaper drinking at Vic's than buying beer at the grocery store. But sometimes we'd load a sidecar to our beers: a bourbon on the rocks for me, scotch for Dockins, sometimes martinis. Those days are a little foggy. This particular day we'd been at the bar since noon and the after-work rush had come in at around 5:30. Who knows what Dockins and I had been talking about? Maybe it was Dockins's theory that iambic pentameter is not the "natural rhythm of the English language," because most words, according to those Dockins would offer up while sitting at the bar, were trochaic: window, sidecar, barstool, ashtray, liquor, bourbon, whiskey, vodka, etcetera. A group of four beautiful young professional women walked in and ordered drinks then stood in a circle in the middle of the bar, sipping said drinks and talking. Any rational (i.e., not drunk) man would see that this was an after-work girl group clearly having girl time, and they would not be interested in men hitting on them. But not me. I wouldn't recognize this, not after a sidecar or two. They were a couple brunettes, a blonde, and a dirty-blonde, in heels and form-fitting suit pants and skirts, their hair did, makeup and jewelry on, clearly still dressed from the law firms, or consulting or banking offices in which they worked. I had to step up to this group of beautiful women, lean into their circle, sniff audibly, and utter the ridiculous lines that head this paragraph. It was so bad that even the bartender (who knew me well) had to yell across the busy bar, "Jesus, Jamie. Sit your ass down." And, other than the looks of disgust and impatience that crossed these women's faces, the bartender's response was the only response my oh-so-cool line generated. Failed, I returned to my barstool next to a laughing Dockins. I ordered another sidecar.

Nice coinslot . . .

Vickery's again. In fact, you will be little surprised that these stories about pickup lines are often set in bars. The bar was rectangular, horseshoe-shaped. Everything was wood-paneled. Other than that they allowed smoking, which at this time did not bother me, because I smoked. It was a pretty cozy place. The food was good, not that I ate it much. I was there for the drinks. Anyway, this time I was near blind-drunk. I'm actually surprised I even remember this. I think I remember it because of how shameful it is. What a jackass I can be. There was this Filipina hanging out with a white guy at the bar. It was getting towards closing time, and I'd been there for a while. Dockins wasn't even with me. I was alone. At this time Vickery's had a cigarette machine sitting just inside the foyer when you walked in the front door, and I had sauntered over to buy a fresh pack of Camels. This petite girl was cute and it was summertime, so she wore a tight yellow t-shirt that showed off every curve, and a pair of lowriding jean shorts. They weren't quite daisy dukes, but they were close, and as I passed I noticed she had a bit of plumber's crack showing. I thought that was just funny. It was obvious that the guy she was with wasn't her boyfriend. They were chatting, sitting next to one another, but there didn't seem to be any romantic tension, and no affection (in that way) passed between this couple. Why are we so unlucky that alcohol makes us do such stupid things? We'd exchanged a few pleasantries, since it was only us three sitting at the bar. So, I guess I felt that some kind of rapport had been built. I got my cigs and the fifty cents change that the machine dispersed, and as I walked behind this little Asian girl with her ass crack hanging out I slipped a quarter between her cheeks and said, "Nice coinslot. But if I had a Cheeto, I'd put that in there." Well you can imagine how well this move went over. The girl was mad, her guyfriend was mad, the bartender was mad. I was laughing. The guyfriend—really, I'm surprised he didn't just sock me in the face—held up his arms and pleaded with me, saying, "Come on, man, that's pretty goddamn rude, and you should apologize." So I did, and then I felt really bad. Somewhere in there I was still laughing a little, and I still laugh awkwardly inside when I think about what I did. But it's an awkward laugh because I was such a fuckup and such a drunk, and it was a good thing that a few years later I cleaned myself up.

**Woman: You're smart, wearing shorts out here. I'm really hot.
Me: Well, you're right about one thing: you *are* hot.**

This one wasn't really a pickup line either, as I never intended for it to go anywhere. It just occurred to me for whatever goddamn reason as I was walking through downtown Atlanta one day in March or April—that time in spring when no one knows what to wear because the weather doesn't know what the fuck to do. Still, Jesus, when I think back on that, what kind of bullshit was I spouting? She was, in fact, an attractive woman, and it was warm outside, and she wore a sweater and pants. I was on my way to the train station and we were walking up Marietta Street and she saw me in the reflection of storefront windows, about to pass her in my shorts and t-shirt when she said the above line. If I wasn't an idiot I might've seen that this was actually a line she was delivering to me, or at least an honest observation from a gregarious person. If I wasn't an idiot I might've recognized that this beautiful woman was actually attempting to start a conversation with me, of all people. But no, I am an idiot, so I had this spontaneous and stupid retort form at my lips and leave them, a little love note scribbled on a paper airplane and tossed only to land, very likely, in the garbage bin of this woman's memory. Immediately after this jawdropper, which is what happened—I briefly noted—I crossed the street, on to the subway, and out of that woman's life forever. Oh, Casanova.

Can daddy have a kiss?

The only pickup line—if you want to call it that—that I use anymore. If you've ever known any one-and-a-half year-old little girls then you know that you've got to tease affection out of them, if it ever comes at all. Children at this age are, understandably, self-centered. Still, my daughter is a sweetie. Let's say that I'm biased, but I think my daughter has a good heart. I've seen her in daycare when one of the other kids was crying, and my girl went to the other kid's cubby hole to retrieve her stuffed animal then walked it over to her. I assume she did this because she put it together that this other toddler was sad and having her stuffed animal might make her feel better. You can tell that I'm no model human. I've got my share of problems and have had moments of, shall I say, less than stellar behavior. Over the years I put a squash on my excessive drinking and I don't do drugs anymore. The result of those changes in my activities was garnering a wonderful lifelong mate. With that mate I chose to procreate and this one-and-a-half-year-old is the result of that choice. I know that probably the best thing I can do for this sweet little girl is shower her with all the love I can. Me, I'm a sucker, and sometimes I want a little in return. To my daughter's credit, she rations her devotions. This gives me hope that she will fare far better as a human than I have.

How Unattractive People Really Are

This late spring/early summer my wife and I invested in a membership at Atlanta's Piedmont Park Conservancy, and, concurrently, the Piedmont Park Pool. So far, this has been wonderful, as it's already topping ninety degrees and sixty percent humidity here in what people sometimes call "Hotlanta." We did this because our daughter is nearing one year old, and we knew that she'd like the pool, and it would give us plenty to do on the weekends, or in the weekday late afternoons, if I want to pick our baby up from daycare early. And we can wear the kid out, as it's a very kid-friendly pool, with a beach entry, and the whole thing never gets deeper than four feet, and she can bounce and splash around and generally make herself sleep-ready.

So far, what's been great is getting down to the pool, dropping off my wife and baby, going for a three-mile jog then returning to the pool, changing into my swim trunks, and dunking into that lovely water. But the other thing that's great about the pool is people-watching. And I'll admit that since I'm a guy, I'm always interested in seeing women in their bathing suits.

But I've been surprised at how average-looking everyone at the Piedmont Park pool is. For the unfamiliar, Piedmont Park and its pool are located in Midtown Atlanta, a neighborhood roiling with "beautiful" people. At the park on a warm weekend, one sees so many hardbodies you'd think you accidentally stepped into a fitness magazine's photo shoot. Abs jog along the concreted and graveled paths. Everyone playing volleyball does so in bikini and Speedo, and does so gracefully, beautifully. And at the pool, there's no shortage of these hardbodies. The thing is, while I'm walking or jogging in the park, I never have the opportunity to really *look* at these bodies, not like I've had the opportunity to do while at the Piedmont Park pool.

What I've seen are certainly beautiful people: men tall and sculpted, women curved and tanned. But what I've also seen are all the little imperfections: curdled thighs, sagging breasts (both male and female), wrinkles, weathered leather for skin. Too many hours spent exercising, tanning, being "beautiful."

It's important I point out that I myself am the farthest thing from "beautiful" you can probably imagine. I'm overweight (six feet tall, 240 pounds), bearded, red-headed (going gray), and red-bearded (still red). Irregular patches of hair sprout on my shoulders, and squirrel across my chest. I have a triangle of hair on my back at the base of my neck that looks a little like a triangle of pubic hair, and my wife and I humorously refer to this patch as my "back pussy." I'm covered with freckles. I look like an overgrown hobbit. Another thing to mention is that I've long accepted my looks and I deal with this, and no one seems to talk shit, but if they did . . . No, not really. I'm not a violent person. I'm just okay with who I am. I exercise to stave off the inevitable heart problems I'm sure to endure in coming years.

I like submerging in the pool after my jog and searching out my wife and seeing her in the water, cradling my baby, and for a moment I don't recognize either of them, and I think, "Whoa, that woman's cute." I like that no one seems to care that I am not one of the "beautiful" people. I like that the "beautiful" people aren't all that beautiful.

A man sidles up next to me and my family, his pecs solid, squared, tapering into the firm outline of his waist, his oblique abdominals leading like arrows to the *rectus abdomini* which stick out with spaces that cast actual fucking shade on his skin. He smiles, crooked toothed grin, says hello, his voice effeminate, high-pitched, bashful. A large-breasted woman bends at the waist, the rolls of her when-standing-flat belly doubling over, tripling, like a snake's coils in the tones of her skin. Again she stands, resplendent, navel-pierced, auburn coif bunned atop her head, above her Gucci sunglasses. A man plays with his sons, his black skin straining with muscles and ridiculous tattoos: a crucifix, old English-stylized font for text: "I Am One of God's Children"; some kind of tribal-looking pattern rounding a bicep; Asian ideograms drawn down a line on a shoulder blade; flames—as if the man's right arm alone moves at friction-inducing speeds. I realize that it is in fact possible for one human to contain on one body all of the worst and most clichéd of tattoos. When this same man rises from the blue murk to chase down an errant boy, the paunch of his gut falls over his swim trunks' waistband like a flopping piece of wet laundry.

At the snack bar they peddle only the worst of food and drinkstuffs: sodas (or, since we're in the South: *cokes*)—syrups mixed with carbonated water—dispensed over ice; tiny plastic vials of "sports" drinks loaded with refined sugars; hot dogs—the foodstuff of choice apparently—ketchup and mustard-lined, relished, onioned; microwaved personal cheese and pepperoni pizzas which parents slice into edible bits for their children; potato chips (barbecue, sour cream and onion, jalapeño—this last of which I tried and found to be delicious); processed and prepackaged ice cream and popsicle treats; the gamut run of Hershey's candy bars; Uncrustables peanut butter and jelly sandwiches, of which my wife partakes and shares with our daughter who leans into me, peanut butter breath.

Still the majority of families come poolside replete with provisions. In the last fifteen minutes of every hour a lifeguard (himself or herself *almost* attractively sculpted, but also displaying the odd wrinkle, the chubbed gut or buttock) sounds a whistle that comically sings, drops an octave and gradually rises again to a screech—not unlike some sort of militarily-driven call to march—and immediately thereafter booms, "Adult Swim!" The call sends children groaning for the nearest poolside exit, some of them lingering, blow-up beach balls and arm-floaties with them, in the water until a lifeguard blows the whistle again, exclaiming, "Children out!"

At this point the few adults unencumbered by offspring take to the laned and buoyed section for exercise, or float around aimlessly, taking in the calm, as calm is what describes the water: two minutes earlier it boiled with the splashing of a hundred kids. Now, these children have retreated to the chairs and tables their parents have staked out—and this is no small feat, as, for whatever reason, the Piedmont Park Pool is in want of shade, and the few umbrella-ed and tabled areas families snatch up come the 10:00 AM opening hour, and such spaces are coveted not unlike parking spaces arranged nearby one's shopping destination and in the shade of a delicate annual set into a desolate earthen island—and at these stations the adults dole out an abundance of in-between-healthy-and-not delicacies: hummus and pita, potato and pasta salads, a wealth of watermelon, baloney and turkey-and-cheese sandwiches, potato chips, Pringles, Doritos, Funions. Coca-Cola. Dr. Pepper. Ice cold bottled water. The American Abundance.

All these nice people are all so average looking. They slip their shorts back over their swimsuits before they leave. Raise their arms through their T-shirts and tank tops. It's amazing what this clothing does: all these little imperfections again hidden. But for the glorious moment these people, like me, left them bare. We were all gazelles at the one waterhole for miles around. Maybe we were more like chimps. Maybe more like humans.

The Gods of California and North Carolina Fistfight in Heaven

I was raised a Catholic in a small parish in a small town on California's central coast. Unlike what you hear about Catholics and Catholic priests and their various scandals in the media, my experience was very boring. Every Sunday morning my parents roused me, my brother, and my sister, got us dressed, and together we all attended mass. On weekdays after school we attended Catechism at Richard's Hall, beside Our Lady of Refuge. Neither during mass nor in Catechism do I remember the subject of homosexuality coming up.

We weren't ignorant of homosexuality. My uncle, my mother's brother, son to my grandmother and grandfather—the most devout Catholics I've ever known—was gay. Not only is my uncle openly gay, he's an advocate for LGBT rights. And still, during my childhood and today, I'm pretty sure my uncle considers himself Catholic.

This morning I listened to NPR, appalled as the sound bites rolled in from North Carolina after the announced results on the passage of Amendment 1, which banned same sex marriage and civil unions by amendment to the state constitution. I listened as a woman at a gathering cut into a wedding cake. "We are celebrating," this woman said, "because it's now acknowledged what a marriage truly is, and that is between a man and a woman."

It's been years now that same-sex marriage—either its acceptance or abolition—has been a hot topic in American media. Massachusetts legalizes it, Georgia bans it, California legalizes then repeals that legalization, then upholds the legalization. Often, leading the charge against same-sex marriage are religious conservatives, and those favoring equality in the right to marriage are political liberals. What you never hear about are the moderates. In particular, you never hear about religious moderates.

This isn't about acknowledging same-sex marriage, although in order to be forthright on my position: I favor equality in rights for all people, no matter whom they love. Instead, I want to show that while some religious fervently oppose the expression of such a right, not all religious feel that way. The problem is that you never hear about these people in the media. My guess is that it's because they're boring. A Christian, Muslim, Jew—whatever—who's willing to acknowledge that people ought to be able to marry whomever they love simply doesn't make as good a news story as the vitriolic woman wielding a knife and slicing through her wedding cake of oppression.

As a boy my mother explained that my uncle's lover was his roommate. This seemed good enough an answer as to why they were always together. We called him Uncle Roy. We loved seeing them, because Uncle Roy was hilarious and we rarely saw them at all, since they lived in Southern California. Roy was always cracking jokes, and he was an artist, and we'd plead for him to draw us pictures—my brother as a Teenage Mutant Ninja Turtle, my sister as a regal princess, me upon the pitcher's mound. Uncle Matt and Uncle Roy lived in Santa Monica, and we were all situated in northern California, a seven-hour drive away. So we didn't see them often, but when we did it was always a family gathering, usually at my grandparents' house in the Napa Valley. Aunts and uncles, my cousins, Uncle Matt and Uncle Roy. We all went to the pool down the street during the hot summer months, during which we'd celebrate my August birthday under the wood lattice that shaded us. Easters we hunted eggs after mass at Saint Helena Catholic Church. They were happy times, and I was happy to see my uncle and his partner whom I did not know was his partner.

By the time I was old enough to realize that it was odd for two grown men to have been "roommates" for so long, when I asked my mother and she laughed and said, "Oh, honey, they're gay; I thought you knew," it made sense. I thought, *Of course they're gay, duh.* And I didn't care that they were gay. In fact, it would have been creepy if Mom insisted they were heterosexual and still "rooming" together. And it would've made me sad if my Uncle Matt and my Uncle Roy had separated. They were a unit no different than my parents. Shortly after this age my uncles were comfortable enough to openly express their love for each other in front of me and my siblings, and they'd kiss on the lips, and no one ever felt uncomfortable about it (or at least I never did, and no one ever said they felt uncomfortable). When California legalized same-sex marriages, my uncles were among the first to get their marriage license and celebrate their legal union. I received pictures of the ceremony in my Gmail.

Legally, it wasn't always like this in California. The state's history is Catholic. Franciscan friars were the first Europeans to set permanent feet on the soil, and their position on homosexuality was decidedly conservative. I learned this while writing a book about the state's colonial history, and about my life growing up as a Catholic there. Here's an excerpt:

> Among the Ohlone of Santa Clara the padres were astonished to find men who dressed and acted like women. The fathers, investigating, asked other Californians, who assured the Franciscans that indeed some men preferred to be considered as women. Fathers Fray Tomás Peña and Joseph Murguía, along with armed corporals, detained one individual, undressing her to determine her sex and upon discovering his penis, forced him at gunpoint to don the clothing of other male Indians, which was nothing at all. They kept the transvestite native at Mission Santa Clara against his will, ashamed of his nakedness, for the Ohlone women did not go naked as the men did. They forced him to perform menial tasks such as sweeping the mission plaza. This poor native was told that he should not dress as a woman and that he should live among god-fearing men in sin. Then, finally, the

priests allowed the man to leave. Later reports assured the fathers that his conduct persisted as before. Further investigation turned up *coias*—as the natives called men who dressed as women, and who were the wives of other men—in tribes throughout the region. When the missionary fathers saw two neophyte men—one dressed as a woman—enter a *reduccion* dwelling together, the Spaniards accosted them and found the two engaged in acts that would surely offend a Catholic God. The padres punished the men, though the one protested that his partner was his wife, and the Franciscans replied with instructions against the most execrable sin these men had been committing. The friars hoped that with the spread of a Catholic God in the area, such evil and detestable people would be eradicated and in their stead adherents to the fold of the Holy Faith would reign for the greater good of all those native and degraded people.

But I grew up in a very different California. My mother tells me that my grandparents went through a transition period where they learned to deal with the fact of their son's sexuality. But as a kid I couldn't have known that. My grandfather laughed at Roy's jokes, and my grandmother leaned in to hug and kiss both of them when they left to head south at the end of their visit. We sat together at the same table for meals, prior to which we took hands and chanted "Bless us, oh Lord for these our gifts . . ." Then my grandfather would bless all the dead dogs and we sat together and ate, my gay uncles and the rest of us.

And of course I can only imagine what the "transition" was like for my uncle, as he decided to come out to his Catholic family. How he must've been afraid, how he must've forced himself to be strong about who he was.

My parish priest was Father Scott McCarthy, a rather tall man, with long red hair and a big red beard. When he wasn't covered in his vestments for mass, he usually sported Birkenstock sandals, khaki shorts, and a tie-dyed t-shirt. For three months out of every year he left us to live with the Sioux in Wyoming, where he preached to them and was granted honorary tribal membership. Yes, this was a *Catholic* church that I attended, and Father Scott was a Catholic priest.

I fulfilled the Sacraments: Baptism, Holy Communion, Reconciliation, Confirmation. I'm married now, but I was not married in a Catholic ceremony, so technically I'm not sure I've committed that Sacrament. While we didn't talk about homosexuality with Father Scott, I remember asking him why there were so many different kinds of churches. My best friend, Randy, was Presbyterian. We'd visited relatives in England who were Anglicans. The funny men who sweated in their gaudy suits on TV on Sunday afternoons called themselves Baptists. Why, in the Apostle's Creed, does it say, "I believe in the holy Catholic church"? What did God think about all these other churches, and which one was right? I must've been eight or nine years old. Father Scott smiled at me and said, "There are many ways to love God, and God loves all His creatures." And that settled it. It seemed like a pretty darn good answer to me. Why would God care how people loved him as long as they did?

When I went away to college and began reading Descartes and Nietzche and Darwin and many other thinkers, and I questioned the faith under which I'd been brought up all my life, I told my family about it and we had stimulating conversations on the subject of God and history and evolution and indoctrination. My sister, who was in Catechism for her confirmation at the time, told her class and Father Scott about my questions, about my challenges to the tenets of Catholicism. Father Scott smiled—as he always did—and said, "Many times throughout your life your faith will be challenged. These challenges help your faith to grow." When I picked up my sister from the parish house that evening, after her class had ended, Father Scott smiled at me and shook my hand, said how nice it was to see me. I only learned what my sister had told them on the drive back home, and so I was embarrassed. But now, looking back, I'm overcome by the class, dignity, and character of Father Scott.

Father Scott moved on from Our Lady of Refuge and took on another flock in some other parish. I have only my memories of his kindness. But if I could talk to him about my uncles and gay marriage, and about my own, non-Catholic marriage, I imagine that it would go something like this:

Father Scott: Do you love your wife?

Me: Yes.

Father Scott: Then I'd say you've committed to the Sacrament of Holy Matrimony.

Me: My uncles are gay and are also married, and my Uncle Matt's a Catholic.

Father Scott: There are many ways for people to express their love for one another, and God loves all His creatures.

Why We Need Superheroes, or, A Parental Theory, or What Was Just A Review of *Chronicle* Before People Were Murdered While Watching *The Dark Knight Rises*

I wrote this essay and revised it, revised it some more, and let it sit then came back and reread it, and thought, yes, this essay has shaped up nicely and I like what I've got to say about superheroes and why we like their stories. Then twelve people were murdered and fifty-eight wounded by a lone gunman in a movie theater during a showing of the latest Batman movie. Some (admittedly iffy) reports have claimed the suspected gunman, James Holmes, called himself "The Joker" when police apprehended him. Holmes apparently liked superhero movies and was obsessed with Batman. Police reportedly found a Batman mask in his booby-trapped apartment. Of course fiction is fiction and we cannot lay blame for this person's crimes on a story or that story's actors, writers, directors. Millions of people watch violent films and television without ever committing a crime. And, obviously, horrendous crimes were committed in bygone eras devoid of such modern theatrics. But, no matter how tangentially Batman might be related to these crimes, I could not go on writing an essay about superhero stories—including the movies based on those stories—without referring to this act of senseless violence.

So now what do I have to say about why we love superhero stories? We love them more—and perhaps we feel we need them more—than ever.

But before all that happened, this July my wife, daughter, and I had just visited my family in California and on our return flight to Atlanta my wife and I met with a reprieve when our one-year-old fell into a deep sleep in our arms. She didn't even wake when my wife had to use the bathroom and shifted the baby into my lap. I took this quiet opportunity to scan the movie offerings on those individual screens that some Delta flights afford passengers. The movie choices are not usually very good and the descriptions of the plots are vague, especially if you're like me and you hardly watch television and so remain ignorant when it comes to pop culture. I ended up selecting one of these vague choices, with an equally vague title. I didn't know anything about *Chronicle*. The plot synopsis was something like "three friends chronicle their lives through a camcorder when suddenly everything changes." I didn't recognize the actors' names, and I think that's why I chose it; I figured I'd try something completely unknown.

I got lucky. The movie is not very long (at eighty-three minutes it's closer to the length of movies that I grew up on and not the typical two-hour epics that are common today), and I didn't know when my daughter might wake, which would end my movie-watching experience. But she snoozed right through the whole thing, and afforded me the time to think about the ideas that coalesced in writing the first draft of this.

The story is about three high school kids who stumble upon some mysterious object buried underground that, when they get close to it, gives them powers that they spend the rest of the movie learning how to use until one of them goes off the deep end and . . . well, the plot really isn't important. What's important is that, aesthetically, superhero stories are my guilty pleasure: I love them, even though I know that, generally, they are juvenile, formulaic, and poorly written. And though I love them, I don't write them. And I like to read and/or watch them, but I don't talk about them like I would talk about the more literary reading that I do, and I would never mention a superhero movie when talking about film with my friends, because we're usually talking about some pretty highbrow stuff. (Since I'm a writer, and most of my friends are writers, the last conversation I can remember having about movies was about Kenneth Anger's *Invocation of My Demon Brother*.) But why should I be ashamed that I like superhero stories? What's wrong with that? Or is there nothing wrong with it? Is there something deeper about superhero stories, or about me, or about all of us, that I wasn't acknowledging?

As a kid I read Superman and Batman comics and around the age of ten or eleven "graduated" to what my peers called the "not lame" Marvel comics, in particular the X-Men, and from there I gravitated into a love of all things Wolverine. Yeah, I am a cliché. While I never really read Spider-Man or any other Marvel universe comics—or any other DC comics, for that matter—on Saturday mornings I watched the *Super Friends*. I watched the old Adam West *Batman*. I saw all of the original Star Wars movies in the theater and was enamored with the Jedi. I saw all the *Superman* movies, too. I was right there when the Tim Burton *Batman* opened, and I've seen every incarnation of Batman since, except this new one, which I've yet to see. I've been to the openings of all the X-Men movies. None of these comics or cartoons or television shows or movies was particularly "good." I don't think any of their authors, directors, actors, etcetera, deserve Nobel Prizes or Emmys or Academy Awards. Although maybe Heath Ledger deserved his Oscar for his Joker performance. He *was* up against Phillip Seymour Hoffman, but the point is that superhero stories are still good solid fun, no matter how silly or preposterous they might be.

But why? What draws me to these stories? Is it the oft-cited superhero's rugged individualism and resourcefulness that Americans are naturally enamored with? Is it the fantasy of being more powerful than I can imagine, which I desire because I am so weak? Is it the simple joy of the imagination inspired by the fantasy of obtaining such abilities?

It's obvious that these stories have been popular for decades and remain so today. I mean, I'm not the only one who likes them. Just look at the smattering of summer blockbusters that feature superhero characters: *The Avengers, The Amazing Spider-Man, The Dark Knight Rises*. But everyone already knows that superhero stories are popular.

Many have written about superheroes and why audiences are attracted to them. In a comic strip written by Mike Russell that appeared in *The Oregonian*, two superhero-enamored kids discuss—very eruditely—why people love superhero movies: there have been superhero movies almost as long as there have been superhero comics, the stories are ready-made for epic-scale dramas, they're made from simple good-versus-evil plots, along with the super power fantasy, they feature corporate-owned characters that can be reinterpreted whenever so that sequels and reboots can be made *ad infinitum*, and they're ripe for marketing tie-in toys, games, clothing and costumes, IMAX and 3-D theater versions, etcetera.[1]

And, recently, Seth Stevenson, covering the 2012 Comic-Con for *Slate*, attended an academically-oriented panel discussion wherein college professors (notably, Ben Saunders from the University of Oregon and Robin Rosenberg, a clinical psychologist) discussed the reasons why we love these costumed crusaders. Not surprisingly, these academes brought up Carl Jung and Otto Rank, whose work on the cultural phenomenon of the mythological hero's journey informs virtually every culture's storytelling, from Moses and Hercules to Superman and Batman.[2]

The stereotypical comic book reader is male and nerdy. He may be overweight or skinny. He is not usually athletically gifted. He has social issues, like anxiety, or awkwardness, and has few friends. I guess that in my life I have both exhibited and defied this stereotype. I loved to read, and I was often labeled a "dork," or a "nerd" by those who did not read as much, or who did not excel academically, and often it happened that these tormentors were from the reigning Hispanic demographic. The other white kids were also often called "dorks" and "nerds." I know that in reality nerdiness was not cut across racial lines, but in childhood it seemed that way. But I wanted to be socially accepted. I played sports, and while I was

---

[1] http://www.oregonlive.com/movies/index.ssf/2012/07/web_comic_why_do_we_love_super.html
[2] http://www.slate.com/articles/life/dispatches/features/2012/comic_con_2012/comic_con_2012_why_batman_is_more_popular_than_superman_right_now_.html

not a great athlete, I was also not a completely uncoordinated waste of space on the baseball diamond or football gridiron. Brief moments of athletic magic visited me. I kept much of my nerdy reading to myself by doing it at night when I couldn't sleep, and I kept quiet in the classroom, and did not always raise my hand to answer my teachers' questions. I started hanging out with Hispanic kids, dressing like them and talking like them. By the time high school came around I was beginning to develop my own identity and the divisions (both socially and racially) softened, or dissolved, a bit. I returned to my friendships with some of my white and "dorky" friends, and at the same time I kept my friends who were jocks and I maintained the friendships I'd built with the Hispanic kids. I was popular enough to go to all the cool kid parties, but I still kept my "nerd" friends.

I paint this picture so that I can say that, while some people love superheroes and superhero stories because they represent a fantasy in which powerless people (skinny and fat nerds who are social rejects) gain power and acceptance due to their exceptional abilities, that wasn't necessarily the case for me. I was overweight, but I channeled that weight into lifting weights for football, and so I grew strong, even if still chubby, and I was intimidating enough that no one really wanted to fight me, if that was ever going to happen, which it didn't because I was a pretty nice person. And because I was nice I was not a social reject, despite my "nerd" tendencies, which I repressed enough to be socially popular, but not enough to get bad grades. So I cannot say I shared the fantasy of living vicariously through a character that is seemingly all powerful.

I was also a Catholic, and I heard about and read the stories of Joseph in Egypt, after his brothers sold him into slavery; and Moses, who led the Israelites to the Promised Land; and Jesus of Nazareth, who despite his humble birth, grows up to perform great miracles and save everyone in his death through crucifixion.

Roger Ebert, in his review of 2009's *Watchmen*, remarked on the modern superhero's roots in ancient cultures' mythologies, even down to their iconic accoutrements (e.g., Zeus's lightning bolts, or Hermes's winged sandals) and their archetypal adventures (Odysseus's travels to the underworld; Jesus' 40-day-and-night banishment to the desert).[3] So, Wolverine has his trademark claws, and Luke Skywalker must face Darth Vader before he's a true Jedi. Some comic book/movie superheroes literally *are* ancient mythological gods, such as Thor. And even non-god super characters refer to themselves in godly terms at times, as when Magneto tells Pyro that he is "a god among insects" in *X-Men 2*.

Here's my point: I like superheroes and superhero stories because they are a democratic society's version of mythology, and are stories about gods, goddesses, demigods, and demigoddesses. Thus, by extension, they are stories that comfort us because they tell us how to act in life, and because they serve this function they are a kind of parental "voice" for the collective consciousness.

Gilgamesh is so powerful that he can haul hundreds of pounds of armor and weapons for thousands of miles in just a few days, and he can then slay outrageous monsters just for the hell of it. He is part god, and part human. So he cannot outlast death. Try as he does, he cannot

[3] http://rogerebert.suntimes.com/apps/pbcs.dll/article?AID=/20090304/REVIEWS/903049997

achieve immortality. So, even though he performs superhuman feats, he more closely resembles us than anything else. And in his failed quest for immortality he provides a powerful lesson to his people that resonates with readers of the epic in our era. He returns to Uruk to act as a benevolent king, to raise the city walls in which he tells his and Enkidu's story, and, ironically, through storytelling, he achieves the immortality he so vainly sought.

YHWH, of Old Testament fame, is an all-powerful, all-knowing god. But, he's not perfect. He creates the universe and Earth, and all living things, but he kind of screws up when he sees that Adam is lonely, so he creates Eve to pacify him (that is, depending on which of the two creation myths in Genesis you want to subscribe to, in this case the one where he first creates Adam, then Eve out of Adam's rib, and not the other, where he creates humans, male and female he created them, i.e., at the same time). Whoops, God made the mistake of giving his human creation free will, so *bam*: original sin. Anyway, there are many instances of YHWH being not-so-perfect: he gets angry and kills all life on earth, then regrets having done that, and he forgets his covenant with the Israelites, and on and on. Still, the characters of the Old Testament look to their "Father in heaven" for protection, for guidance, for education, for sustenance.

The bloodshed at the end of the *Odyssey*—after all the suitors are dead, and their relatives then seek vengeance against their killers—never would have ended until Odysseus and Telemachus had killed everyone on Ithaca but themselves, had not Athena swooped down from Olympus and raised her goddess voice, and had not Zeus sent a lightning bolt of authority so that Odysseus would obey the goddess. For the ancient Greeks, while they could at once revere and ridicule their gods and goddesses, ultimately they relied on them for supreme guidance.

As Nietzche said, "God is dead." Welcome to the 21st century. Of course, realistically, for many people their god is certainly *not* dead, but due to our (I mean American) Constitutional freedom of religious expression, our government "shall make no law respecting an establishment of religion, or prohibiting the free exercise thereof." And since our culture consists of many cultures, with no one set of cultural values holding any *legal* power over any others, the superhero has become our mythology.

There's the now cliché "with great power comes great responsibility" line from *Spider-Man*, a line that Peter Parker picks up from his surrogate dad and that, through his actions, he passes on to all the young people he saves and who admire him. And there's us, the eager audience, soaking up this hokey truism because, vague and cliché or not, there's some truth there.

That's one example, but in the multiverses of comic lore—as in real life—there are many kinds of parents that tell us many different things about how we ought to live. Superman, with his Truth, Justice, and the American Way motto represents a kind of patsy, pre-WWII American idealism that's difficult to translate to a 21st century world, which is perhaps why the franchise has suffered since long before Christopher Reeve's death. But who knows what the future might hold, as *Man of Steel* rebooted the franchise. Batman has done quite well, probably due to his dark nature—at least in the Frank Miller-Jeph Loeb-Dennis O'Neil-inspired reboot that kicked off with *Batman Begins* in 2005. He's mysterious, brooding, full of wrath and a desire for vengeance. Ultimately, though, he has to put aside his personal feelings for those of Gotham City, i.e., the rest of the world. There's Marvel's Wolverine, the rugged individual, good-to-the-bone-but-antisocial guy. Everyone wishes his dad was Logan—the guy's a lumberjack who smokes cigars and drinks beer—and in terms of his distance from everyone else he's probably hitting not far from the mark for many readers'/viewers' relationships with their fathers. As for female superheroes there's Storm and Rogue and Wonder Woman and Jean Grey. I'll argue that, though the majority of superheroes I allude to here are male, gender or sex isn't as important to the overall parental consciousness that superheroes represent as mythological symbols. That said, it's telling that most superhero movies feature male leads in our patriarchal culture, but that's another essay.

In *Chronicle* we see that the superhero mythos takes the place of traditional parenting, and at the same time espouses those same values. The three friends who gain superhero powers are rogues prior to their solidified bond through the experience that grants them power. You have the stereotypical nerd whose mother is dying of a terminal illness, and his alcoholic, abusive father "supports" his family off his disability as a post-accident firefighter. There's an intellectual who has distanced himself from traditional teenage socialization due to what he perceives as teens' ridiculous desire to fit in and be cool. He's reading Schopenhauer and shit. The last guy is popular, seems like a shoe-in for the class president spot he's running for, and has a cheerleader girlfriend, but he gives up all the social amenities that come with such a position in order to hang out with his new friends. I'm conjecturing here, because we learn the least about this last character, but often people in such situations find themselves desperately lonely, as everyone who clings to them does so only for the accompanying social status that they themselves might gain and so this "leader" finds himself without any "true" friends. That is until he gains secret superpowers with two new buddies and now they all three fly through the air and talk about vacationing in Nepal.

Once these three have discovered their new power they run amok playing with it. For a long segment we see the three protagonists playing pranks on people in a Wal-Mart-like store and in the parking lot, and experimenting with each other as their abilities grow. They scare little girls with teddy bears and blow girls' skirts up with unmanned leaf blowers. Good times. The boys are acting like, well, boys. Boys without a parental figure to give them ethical guidance with their new talents.

Once their power takes them over the edge—literally—one of the three friends steps in to fill this parenting role. *Chronicle*'s rules: they are not to use their power in public, or against living things, and they're not to use it when they're angry.

Of course, as in any superhero story, the rules must be broken (otherwise we have one very short and/or boring superhero story/movie) and this leads to the climax. At the film's end we're left with one of the protagonists who, due to the film's found footage style, provides a parental soliloquy as an ending. While recording a messge into the camera for his fallen fellow (fallen after this character had to take his own friend down to protect the innocent) that he loves him, and he's sorry that he never told him so while he was alive. True to form, this sounds like the voice of human reason: we should all spend time with each other, showing that we love one another, because life is so goddamn short.

As is typical for me when reading or watching any superhero story, I'm aware that the writing isn't all that great and *Chronicle*, while surprisingly fresh compared to its contemporaries, is no exception. However, despite my realization that the writing is wanting, I still enjoyed *Chronicle* while I sat on that 757 as it careened through the air (like the movie's characters) across America with my baby cradled in my lap. And that's when these ideas gelled, as I watched this somewhat ridiculous story and looked down at my daughter's wispy locks, her peaceful closed eyelids, and her little pursed lips. I like superheroes and their stories because I want to feel taken care of. I admit I get a little emotional (and I try to not show this when reading or watching a story like this in public) when Superman—or any other hero—saves his first civilian and I see the look of gratitude on that hapless and helpless citizen's face. There's no hiding my sentimentality, so I just accept it. Superheroes make us feel like there's some benevolent good out there and it will triumph over the evil of the world. These stories teach us that we must be good to one another and that, when we act in such ways, we can defeat all that opposes us, or that we can learn the unknown. And these are the values that good parenting ought to instill.

And that brings me back to James Howell and the Aurora massacre on the opening night of *The Dark Night Rises*. Despite articles citing the film's violence, Batman's cold heartlessness, spurious claims that Howell called himself The Joker, the people were in that theater that early morning (some of them with babies and young children) because they love the myth of the superhero. They were going to see good triumph over evil and they would take comfort in that idea. Unfortunately, evil visited them that very night. But I believe there is still good in the world, and all the James Howells out there cannot defeat it.

When I look at my daughter when she's looking at me, what do I see? In her eyes I read absolute love and devotion, but at the same time I see her exercising her free will, especially when she's been chewing on the buttons of the remote control that she's snatched off the coffee table and I ask, "Can I have that, please?" I also see that she looks to me for protection, when she stumbles to me, arms up for me to hold her when she's fallen and she's crying. In her eyes I see that she needs me for sustenance, when I set her in her highchair and bring to her a snack or meal. I see that she seeks guidance when I read to her before I put her to bed, as with my finger I underline the words, "Goodnight moon," and point to the book's illustration of that yellow cookie-looking thing she's learning all about. I see peace when she's exhausted after her story and I lay her in her crib and she somehow knows, intuitively (call it faith), that she's safe, that I will protect her, and that she can drift off to her dreams. For my daughter, I am her Superman, her Batman, her Wolverine, and right now she needs me. And with truth, justice, and in an ethical way, I will not let her down.

THIS ESSAY CANNOT SLEEP

It's 2:37 in the morning as I write this and I've been awake since 10:00 AM yesterday, after having finally fallen asleep at 7:40 earlier that morning, prior to another sleepless night. If the times in that sentence are hard to figure out, forgive me. Though they seem to make sense to me, I am likely as confused as you. I can't make time of my sleeplessness. Even the utterance of that word, like a hiss, a deflating air mattress, a string of zzzzzzzzzs in a vacuum, no medium or tempo. No time. No sleep.

•

In our medicine cabinet: a bottle of Melatonin, packages of Alka Seltzer Plus Night Cold Formula. In our bedroom closet: a twice-used relaxing sound-generating machine, and some machine called the Nightwave that produces a flashing blue light to which one matches his breathing to relax the body till he drifts off. All failed attempts at drugs or gadgetry to ease my body and mind to sleep.

•

Some of the books that I have read, some in single sittings, when I could not sleep:

Blood Meridian

The Second Sex

Bluets

Child of God

Light Boxes

Nothing: A Portrait of Insomnia

The Gay Science

•

I've had sleep problems since I was a boy. This, in part, made me a reader, as I lay awake nights, a flashlight in one hand, book in the other. Stories unraveled, pages turned. When I did not or could not read my mind turned over stories of its own. From what I remember, most of these were fantasies involving girls. Mostly, these weren't sexual. I remember first being attracted to girls around the first grade, and I'd wish that I and whatever little girl I had a crush on would live some life together that mostly consisted of snuggling in my bed, or on the couch in front of the television. Usually these stories followed the pattern of me doing something heroic to help this little girl out, like rescuing her from a burning building, or defending her when other kids at school made fun of her. Then she'd be attached to me, and we held hands all the time.

•

Once, my family took a two-week-long road trip around the western United States and Canada, and at one point we camped outside of Elko, Nevada on a warm summer night. My father had purchased this Coleman pop-up trailer from a family friend for something like a hundred bucks. To this day my dad's eyes get wistful as he says what a good deal that camper was. We towed this thing that looked like an oversized suitcase when it was collapsed behind our station wagon. When it was popped up, what we slept in was some cross between a tent and a mobile home. At each new campsite, dad enlisted me as we unhitched the camper, lowered the stabilizing legs, and cranked her up. Despite the above-mentioned "stabilizing legs" this trailer shook around like you were in an earthquake whenever anyone rolled over in bed, or got up, or did just about anything. You can imagine what two weeks on the road with your kids might do to your love life if you're said kids' parents. I'd never told Mom and Dad that I had trouble sleeping because I didn't know there was anything weird about it. So I lay there when Mom and Dad started giggling and whispering and the trailer started shaking around like mad. It was plain pointless to continue to lie there. I knew what was going on and I felt uncomfortable. The thought of what my parents were doing made me sick to my stomach. So I got up to leave, which made my parents freeze and Mom asked if everything was okay, and I told her that I needed to use the bathroom, but really I just sat at our campsite's picnic table and stared at the stars over the desert for an hour or so, or at least till the trailer stopped shaking.

•

More books I've read during sleepless nights:

Fast Machine

Suicide

Notes from Underground

No Country for Old Men

About a Mountain

The Collected Plays by Wole Soyinka

•

I remember one Christmas Eve when I still believed in Santa Claus: the excitement, the anticipation! No way I was going to sleep that night. My father put me down in his and Mom's bed, probably knowing that I would not sleep. He said, "Just stay here, and look out the window. You might see Santa and his sleigh." My parents' bed sat below the long narrow window that looked out on the backyard and, from my lying-down position, the sky, clear of fog on this Xmas Eve night. I watched the stars twinkling. I thought about what I'd asked for from Santa (Who knows that year? GI Joes, Transformers, a bicycle?) and how I'd find them beneath the tree in the morning. I lay there thinking and staring at the sky until it grayed, then I leapt from the bed and rushed to our living room. I suppose that my parents slept on the hide-a-bed in the family room's couch but I don't remember. I remember the tree lit up in the dark of the living room, shining on mine and my brother's and sister's toys, those that required assembly already put together, as if Santa had actually built them in his workshop with his elves. I was supposed to wait until everyone was awake until I could open any presents or play with my new toys, and I sat on the steps that led down into our living room for a minute, gazing at the magic of this scene. Then I ran to wake up my brother and sister and the three of us rustled up our groggy parents who promptly put on a pot of strong coffee.

•

Some time after the cat I had as a boy died (my dad accidentally running over her in the driveway) I lay awake in bed thinking about the fact that my parents one day, too, would die, and I was terrified at the prospect of this inevitability. I walked down the hall and found my father reading the newspaper at our dining room table and I was crying and I told him what I was thinking about. Dad said, "Son, calm down. That's many many years from now." I think of this this morning when I lay awake in bed unable to sleep, a couple years after Dad suffered the stroke that has brought him clearly—from my point of view, at least—into old age.

•

It must've been terribly frustrating for my parents and grandparents that I had trouble sleeping. I couldn't sleep at my grandparents' home one night and went to their bedroom and inadvertently interrupted—well. Let's just say that while I'm not scarred or anything, it's best not to have to see your grandparents naked—ever.

•

Books that I am writing/have written and on which I have made great headway because I could not sleep:

This one

The Book of Freaks

The Fat Kid

Prose. Poems. a Novel.

Our Lady of Refuge

Last Mass

The Lake

Metal Penelope

•

Recently the new "video," "8 Hours - Shower Relaxing Water Running Ambient Sounds ducha Dusche duş душ," on Youtube is my currently-working sleep aid. We'll see how long that lasts. Whenever I try something new in an attempt to sleep it works for about one month. I guess that I get used to the sleep aid, like my brain figures out a way to work around it.

•

In high school I started smoking weed, but I also started hanging out with my friends at odd hours of the night, hours during which I'd already have been awake anyway. But now I was stoned. When I rolled in to my parents' house, through the garage door so as not to wake anyone else, all of them snuggled in their beds, I crept to the room I shared with my brother and gloriously fell fast asleep.

•

It's 5:04 AM as I write this. I woke and had to pee. If I'm lucky, my daughter won't be up for another two hours. But I can tell already that I won't be falling back to sleep. I can tell how long I've slept from the eight-hour "Sound of Shower" Youtube video: four hours and forty-four minutes. I don't know this for sure, but I would guess that my average number of hours of sleep per night is somewhere around four.

•

Things I think about when I'm trying to sleep but I cannot: This arm that I injured won't heal up and it's sore when I lie on my right side but I want to lie on my right side goddamn it. Oh shit, I have that meeting about the poetry contest I'm judging. Did I miss that? I should check my phone. Oh good, that's not till Thursday. Sex. What was that sound? Neighbors? Yeah, probably the neighbors. Tomorrow I have to buy plane tickets, send a transcript and a resume, work on edits and revisions, try to do other writing, go jogging. I need to stop eating such shitty food. If I just stopped eating shitty food I might actually lose some weight. Sex.

•

Alka Seltzer Plus Cold Night Formula contains doxylamine succinate, an antihistamine that by itself or in combination with codeine, is often used as a sedative. This is the chemical that would sometimes make me drowsy and lull me to sleep when I actually was sick, and an aid I have used when I was not suffering a cold. I try not to rely on such measures, though.

•

I once read that Napoleon Bonaparte was an insomniac, that he slept in fifteen-minute naps every few hours, which helped with his brilliant military strategy, but his years of insomnia—for all we know—also could've compounded, the effects contributing to his failures at Waterloo.

•

According to Wikipedia, lights-out baseball refers to "A pitcher who so dominates the hitters that the game is effectively over once he takes the mound—so they can turn out the lights and go home. The pitcher retires the batters in order without allowing a single run." And some baseball announcers have been known to say "Good morning, good afternoon and good night" when describing a batter's hitless 1-2-3-pitch at-bat: the final strike the pitch that puts the batter to bed.

•

I've never told a doctor about my sleep trouble for fear that he would put me on some sleep aid that might be habit-forming, which is ridiculous, I know, because in college I found the best habit-forming sleep aid ever: alcohol. (Though some of what I just said is not true, as alcohol is a very ineffective sedative, causing one to have to use the bathroom, and causing sleep disruptions and other disorders.) I drank but a little in high school, some Zimas here and there, Keystone Lights. In my freshman year in college I refused to drink, instead toking up my joints, blunts, and bong rips. But by sophomore year I was drinking like everyone else, and the sedative-like effect of that hypnotic—ethanol—lulled me to dreamless and snoring sleep.

•

It's 1:42 AM as I write this, and I believe my "sound of shower" video has run its course. For the last two hours I lay in bed, those soothing sounds dripping in my ears from ear buds, and nothing. Instead I have an itch on my back, just beneath the shoulder blade. Then my calf itches, then my ankle. Now the itch has migrated to my temple and my neck. I think my curriculum vitae looks pretty good now. The Tables in Microsoft Word are the stupidest thing ever. I'll read these poems by Mike Young. I should probably be reading instead of being on the Internet. That is, reading a real book. There's the girl who friended me on Facebook who's obsessed with body image and is always posting about how fat she is, and how hard she's trying to not be fat. She's changed her last name, or something. She says she's now an atheist. Good for her.

•

Sometimes it seems like my body and brain do not want me to sleep. I've gone to bed at a normal time, lights out, darkness, the soothing sounds of my wife's deep breathing next to me, and I start drifting off, only for my muscles to tense, my whole body jerking, and I'm suddenly awake—wide awake—as if an intruder had burst into our bedroom and my body instinctively reacted to get me up and moving, reacting to the danger. But there's no danger. This process has occurred in some cases no fewer than three or four times in a row: dozing away then snap! awake! At some point when this happens I resign myself to not sleeping and leave the bedroom to read in the living room.

•

People who claimed to never sleep: Albert Herpin, who had no bed or other furnishings in his home conducive to sleepy time, other than a rocking chair in which he claimed to read the newspaper through the night, "resting," until work began the following day; Thai Ngoc, who claimed to have gone sleepless for thirty-three years after he suffered a fever that irrevocably changed him; and Paul Kern, a WWI soldier shot in the head, which caused the removal of his brain's frontal lobe. He lived another 40-odd years after this, working in the Pensions office in Budapest, without ever sleeping again.

•

It's 1:26 AM and I have now drunk four beers and still I cannot sleep. I have read from Elena Pasarello's *Let Me Clear My Throat*. I have watched two episodes of *New Tricks*. I am into my third episode of *Deadwood*. Still, no sleep. My baby just awakened, crying for water. I took it to her, held her, patted her back. She fell back, naturally, into sleep. It seems there's no amount of hypnotic, sedative—whatever—that can actually work when I cannot sleep. I'm just *UP*.

•

It's 1:54 AM *Deadwood* over, or at least I don't have any more episodes to watch on the Netflix DVD that came in the mail today. That means I'm just up. Fifth beer.

•

2:06 AM: I've now had six beers today and still sleep will not come.

•

It's 3:22 AM. Still no sleep. Now back at reading *Let Me Clear My Throat*. Will finish book tonight.

•

Yet more books read throughout the nights:

Swann's Way

Alcools

The Golden-mouthed

Pilgrim at Tinker Creek

Bicycle

The Myth of Sisyphus and Other Essays

•

One of the things I do a lot when I cannot sleep is spend time on the Internet reading about not being able to sleep. I also read about serial killers, psychopathy, hypnotic drugs, and night terrors. Sometimes I'm reading about psychopaths and serial killers and I begin to worry that I might be one. This is strange, since I've never had the urge to kill anyone. But the impulsive decision-making, risky behavior, and tendency towards alcoholism, all that fits the bill.

•

The worst thing to endure is the night terrors. I lie upon our living room couch, reading. I'm not in bed so as not to disturb my wife who sleeps like a normal person. Finally, a heavy-liddedness overtakes me. It's not quite sleepiness, and more like it's too much to keep my eyes open. I do not get off the couch and make my way for the bedroom, or even to turn off the overhead light. To do so would snap me back to full wakefulness. I make out every distinct detail of the room: the hardwood floors with the patterned inlay that courses the edges near the walls. The map of all the continents, the other map of Lake Tahoe, the satellite image of Monterey Bay. Books and books and books. I feel another human presence. The hollow thud of feet slowly approaching on those hardwood floors. I can't move. Can't sit up. Can't wave my arms about to fend the intruder off. I feel him right next to me, breathing on my almost-sleeping face. He presses a hand to my side. I shoot up to a sitting position, open-mouthed, screaming. I've been sweating. My heart's beating a presto. The room is empty, except for me, my scream, my sweat. I breathe, calm down. I return to my book. Sometimes this process has repeated itself two or three times in one night.

•

My daughter was born at 8:36 PM. My wife had had a C-section delivery, and I went with the baby and the nurses to get her cleaned up while the doctors stitched my wife back together. By the time we'd washed her, dropped that goop in her eyes, diapered and swaddled her, and after we went to the recovery room where Kinsey promptly found Sarah's chest and curled up, when we finally got back to our room, it must've been around 11:30. My wife was understandably exhausted after her thirteen hours of induced labor, and the surgery, and she fell asleep. I sat there, staring into the clear plastic basinet the cradled my daughter, and I watched her breathe and sleep, and I just hoped that she would keep on breathing.

•

I'd like to say that I've found a way to deal with my sleep issues, but I have not, other than accepting that I have them and, thankfully, they don't plague me most of the time. These days I drink moderately. I admit that it helps calm me down after the day of writing, teaching, grading—whatever. I have not ever used a prescription sleep aid, though I'll bet many probably think that I should. I'm not here to say I know anything about this thing or why I haven't dealt with it in a healthier way. I know why: I'm scared. I feel about doctors the same way that I do about salespeople or auto mechanics. I'm also aware that this is completely irrational. It's as crazy as my fear of sharks, or heights, or lightning. But I'm a fan of the definition of "essay" as "an attempt." So I guess what I'm trying to say is that while I might be looking for answers, it's okay if I don't find any. What matters is that I tried to..

•

The longest stretch of poor sleep I've endured is, I think, a time about two years ago, when I slept a total of about six hours in a week. At first I had the general nausea that comes from sleep deprivation. Fatigue. I don't think I jogged at all during that week. After about the fifth day I started seeing things. I'd be walking to the grocery store down the street from my apartment and I kept seeing a lap dog, or maybe a puppy, running up to my ankles. Had you seen me walking through Midtown Atlanta, you'd see me cruising along, then jumping out of the way of nothing, spinning around, searching the sidewalk for that dog that did not exist.

•

I think I'm still looking for that little dog, if that dog is sleep. Sometimes I find it. In fact, to be honest, most of the time these days I do find it. It might have something to do with becoming a father. I've never done anything that tires me out the way being a daddy to a two-year-old girl does. Still, I have a sleepless night approximately once a week. And I worry. There's an increased risk for heart disease associated with insomnia, and I now know that heart disease comes from both sides of my genes: my dad's grandfather's cause of death was heart disease, and my mother's brother suffered through a near-heart attack, after which the docs put a stent in one of his coronary arteries. And now there's the possibility of more stents to keep the blood flowing, to keep him alive. Then there's my mother's heart defect: hydrotrophic cardiomyopathy. This causes the walls of the ventricles to thicken, and can cause sudden cardiac arrest. Awesome.

•

It's 3:49 AM as I write this. Often when I cannot sleep I look in on my daughter. Sometimes she falls asleep with her legs sticking out through the bars of her crib, her arms thrown back behind her head, fingers still grazing the open book splayed out on her mattress. Her stuffed animals and baby dolls heaped in piles to listen to her tell them the story. It would seem that sleep sneak-attacked her. It came up and there was nothing she could do to stop it.

WHERE ALL THE GOOD GUYS ARE

I guess since most of my Facebook friends are liberals (there are a few libertarians, and some token true conservatives) all I hear about in the feed is liberals complaining about the Right and the multiple predictable points of view that the Right espouses. I'm not complaining about this fact, because I myself am liberal, but it seems that, because of the little bubble of my media world, the Right keeps giving men a bad rap. Arizona defines pregnancy as occurring two weeks before conception; some congressman says, "legitimate" rape; a writer on *HTMLGiant* writes an essay about the power of language inherent in a phrase I've heard many men use when talking about "uptight chicks": "That girl needs to get fucked." I could not agree more that many men do and say terrible things, especially when it comes to women. What I don't hear anything about, though, are some of the good things men do or say, or how most boys grow into caring, emotionally sensitive, thoughtful, and responsible men.

I remember when I was a boy and I said things like, "That girl needs to get fucked," or I laughed and agreed when one of my buddies said it. I say, "when I was a boy," but I'm talking about when I was in my mid and late twenties. Most boys don't become men until this latter stage, while women have long been women and act as such. From everything I've seen and heard about human development, females develop faster than males, and in my own experience with my daughter it seems true: she's way ahead of boys who are months older than her in her daycare class. Females make connections between themselves and others and the elements of their world more rapidly than males do. Females take into consideration the potential results of their actions before males do. Enough with abstractions: when I was twenty-three years old, I didn't know what it meant to say something like, "That girl needs to get fucked."

If our politicians serve as indication of this truth, we would all be led to believe that many men do not ever grow out of this juvenile stage of development. Or maybe conservative social ideologies are a kind of retroactive tribal authoritarianism. Some men feel under attack by women, and so join together in solidarity by offering policies that repress women's rights and at the same time bolster the ideologies of patriarchal institutions under the guise of "morality": Christianity, The Boy Scouts of America, good ol' meat-and-potatoes American values.

Despite what my liberal friends report on in the media, my feeling is that most men are moderate, and most men do grow out of such juvenilia. But that also makes such men boring and not media-worthy. Once, while sitting in a graduate seminar on American Modernist Poetry, a female classmate was talking about Gertrude Stein's *Tender Buttons* and the allusions to female-ness, the body, female sexuality, etcetera, inherent in that book-length poem. Another fellow student, and my good friend, a guy who for years through undergrad had been railing against the "bullshit" that he called feminism, started laughing. This was one of those seminal moments in my own life, in my development. I remember listening to this woman talking and thinking that what she was saying was really interesting, because at this young age (I was twenty-three or twenty-four) I had no idea what to do with a text like *Tender Buttons*. And when this guy, my friend—a guy with whom I'd laughed over beers and said things like "That chick really needs to get fucked"—started laughing at this woman, I was embarrassed. I was embarrassed first for the woman, and later for my friend, because this woman stopped talking, looked at my friend and said, "You know, this whole semester I've been putting up with you saying derogatory things about women and feminism, and I haven't said a thing, in the spirit of letting you air your ideas. But I've never laughed at what you thought, even though I wanted to, and it's rude, and I want you to apologize." My friend chuckled a little bit. The rest of the class was silent, including the male professor. But everyone stared at this friend of mine, including me, waiting for what he'd say in return, and his face reddened, then he said he was sorry. That was the last chauvinistic peep out of that guy that semester.

I'm no longer friends with that man. That could be because I moved 2,500 miles away and I lost his phone number and email address. Or it could be because during this time in graduate school I was growing up, and I no longer thought that feminism was silly. In fact, I'm not sure that I ever thought it was, but that seemed to be what the other guys in the English Department thought and I wasn't confident enough to express an alternate male perspective. It's not that hard to find someone if you really want to maintain a friendship, and I know that's true, because years after I'd moved, on a return to the town where I'd earned my Master's, this guy attended my reading while I was on a book tour. Afterwards we had a few beers and caught up. It was a little sad to hear this guy still saying things like, "You fucking pussy," and "What a fag," and "That chick's hot." I was married to a woman who is a corporate lawyer at one of the country's largest firms. My daughter was not yet conceived, but we knew we wanted a baby (no, Arizona, this was *not* yet a pregnancy). I did not then know that I would eventually have a daughter, but I already knew that if I did have one, it was going to be a tough job raising her in a world full of men like that guy. But I also knew that when I looked around me, at nearly all my male friends—my peers—I saw the responsible, thoughtful, emotionally-sensitive and politically-moderate men who would help me, and maybe when she grew up, she'd be strong, and we'd have all helped to make her world a little better.

DEAR KINSEY,

By the time you read this letter your Dear Old Dad might only exist in photographs and videos, a purely digital essence. If I'm lucky—I guess—I'll still live: a ragged, bent, medicated and oversized raisin clinging to his dusty tomes in his stinking armchair, nodding off with my glasses skiing down my nose with the same gravity that pulls down my slumped-forward noggin. If this latter should be the case, and I don't already have one, do me a favor and buy me a chain to hold said glasses around the folds that used to be my neck.

Whatever my condition, know that at the time I write this I am young(er), a bit more fiery, vivacious even. That's probably why I'm writing this to you in the first place, and I hope that you will read this letter at a similarly angsty time in your life. Perhaps you, too, will be angered enough to want to say or do something that you're passionate about or for. Know that while I will begrudge your generation's shitty music and ridiculous clothing and our leaders' uselessness, I've felt this way for most of my life and, yes, I've pretty much always been insufferable.

Right now you are my little girl, not yet two years old. Your favorite thing in the world is Granny Bunny, the stuffed animal you sleep with nightly. Or maybe it's Mommy. You go through phases. Yesterday at the grocery store you couldn't stand for me to push the cart in which you sat. It *had* to be Mommy. Within a week I suspect the entire universe will orbit around Daddy. Maybe what you love more than anything is Elmo. The look on your face when you get to watch *Elmo's World* on the weekend—akin to the expression of comfort one displays upon snuggling under a favorite blanket—shows me the importance of this Muppet in your toddler realm. It's not quite the eye-rolling spiritual ecstasy you displayed upon first trying ice cream, but comfort is not a religious experience, and I recognize that ice cream is as close to god that an almost-two-year-old is likely to get. I imagine you growing up here in your native country, the United States of America. I wonder what you will be angry about when you're a young woman. My hope is that it will be your generation's shitty music and ridiculous clothing. Perhaps you won't be as insufferable as your Dear Old Dad, but such curmudgeonly attitude is evidence of fortitude, a value long lost in the general population.

It's partly because I think about you as a young woman that I set out to read Simone de Beauvoir's *The Second Sex*. I should note that I'm no stranger to feminist theory, having read bell hooks, Judith Butler, Elaine Showalter, and many others while earning my Master's and Doctorate degrees, and in being someone who's generally interested in texts. But I'd never tackled this behemoth: two books, 732 pages. I bought the first edition as a birthday gift for your mother, whom I might add has never read it.

I wanted the hardback English translation to include in a fairly extensive feminist library, for your future benefit. I was ignorant of the reported poor quality of this first translation, and to the "restored" 2010 translation. Still, there's something about owning first editions, in your Dear Old Dad's useless opinion. And—based on reviews of the new translation—the same issues seem to be prevalent for those reviewers as in my reading of this 1953 original. The point is: this is the book we own and I will give it to you, so perhaps what's important to know is that the biggest criticisms seem to be about Beauvoir's views on sex, about which, if you'll stick with me, I'm sure to embarrass you.

It's worth pointing out that I'm writing to you sixty years after *The Second Sex*'s publication. And the book could well be eighty years old by the time you read this letter. I can only sum up those long decades as compound reasons for reading this book and writing about it to you: your grandmothers were mere children when this book was published; they were teenagers when it influenced Betty Friedan to write *The Feminine Mystique* in 1963; in 1973 your grandmothers were newly-married, not yet planning families, and the U.S. Supreme Court decision in Roe vs. Wade made abortion legal in the United States; by 1983 your D.O.D. was six years old, your mom four, and the push for the Equal Rights Amendment—for which your grandmothers campaigned tirelessly—was dead; in 1993 Madonna began her Girlie Show World Tour in support of her *Erotica* album, and the United Nations adopted its Declaration on the Elimination of Violence against Women; and in 2003 the Iraq War began, and President Bush signed into law the Partial-Birth Abortion Ban Act. So far, in 2013 multiple bans on women serving in combat missions have been lifted in the U.S. military, men on a Fox News segment freaked out over reports that more women than ever are the breadwinners in more American households, and Texas recently passed legislation that would restrict abortion after the first twenty weeks, and make it more difficult, in general, for abortion clinics in that state to operate.

So Beauvoir begins *The Second Sex* in her introduction by asking "Is there a problem?" for there had been "voluminous nonsense uttered during the last century to illuminate the problem." And I will say, yes, there is definitely a problem, and furthermore: "The woman problem has always been a man's problem." This last bit, as evidenced by the cronies mentioned above exhibiting their anti-feminism on national television, couldn't be more ample reason for your D.O.D. talking to you now. Just try not to get too weird about the fact that I have a penis.

I said that I'm angry. In recent years it's become virtually impossible for anyone in the state of Mississippi to have an abortion. The *New York Times* runs an article about an eleven-year-old gang raped in Texas, how she "dressed older than her age, wearing makeup and fashions more appropriate to a woman in her 20s," and about the poor rapists' lives ruined and town shattered as a result. Some senator goes public saying that women's bodies somehow "know" when they're being raped and when sex is consensual, disregarding all medical and scientific knowledge as well as common sense in one stroke. I'm mad thinking that I'll fight a never-ending battle against a culture that will teach you to like "girly" things, like the color pink, and princesses, and that these things are less important than sports like football, or an interest in mechanical engineering. I'm mad that, even though I'm a male writing this letter, women writers are grossly underrepresented in the publishing industry. And the numbers of women legislators also do not reflect the fact that women make up more than half our population, to say nothing of what seems to be the larger current issue, that women in full-time positions earn on average nineteen percent less than male coworkers in the same or similar positions. But, of course, you will likely be confounded by this, having grown up in a household with your college-professor-dad and your corporate-lawyer-mom. And there's that whole "your-mother-is-usually-right-about-everything" thing, and that might make you confused about my insistence that growing up aware of the struggle that millions of women have undergone, and continue to endure, is important for your edification.

I do hope that you will enjoy the pure pleasures of life: Elmo; the park and the playground on weekends; Elmo; music to which your body cannot help but move; something else besides Elmo; skiing down a steep mountain slope with the rush of winter air in your lungs. But I hope—dear god I hope—that you won't ever forget that you are smart and important and special for what you think and do, and not for what a culture tells you that you *ought* to be. So, Kinsey, let me tell you what I think—and no, the irony's not lost on me—about this book, *The Second Sex*.

First, let me tell you how smart Simone de Beauvoir was. The author of over twenty books—novels, essays, political tracts, biographies, and philosophy—she is considered a foundational thinker for contemporary feminism. She died in 1986, just two years after the above-mentioned state of Mississippi finally ratified our country's 19th Amendment, which ensured women the right to vote. This book, *The Second Sex*, Beauvoir researched and wrote in fourteen months, and if you've ever tried writing *anything* you probably recognize that this is amazing. First published in French in 1949, and translated by H.M. Parshley in 1953, this is the edition of the book you own. But, according to many critics, Parshley cut great portions of the original text and translated some sentences poorly, just a like a man would.

Among the things I was interested to learn about was how relevant the information and argument of this book would be in 2013. I'm disappointed to report that much of it does hold up, but at the same time I'm delighted that parts of it seem so antiquated that I pictured women in crinoline Victorian dresses, with corsets and bustles, though Beauvoir wrote in an era at least sixty years beyond such inhibiting fashions. In other words, it's totally cool for you to wear jeans, but it's also largely acceptable that, should you wear form-fitting jeans, our patriarchy might consider you a "slut." Of course, if you've ever read anything by your D.O.D. prior to this you are likely confused as to what's meant by "slut," because I regularly write about being one myself.

I could go on and on about how disturbing all of this is, but I think it's probably better if I rely on a pathos appeal and so shall endeavor to embarrass and laugh you into agreement with my perspective. If you ever read this you'll likely be an adult by then, so here goes:

The beginning of *The Second Sex* covers the biological differences between men and women. Dudes are dicks. They are hubristic, conceited, domineering but insecure, and in some cases, misogynistic. You will have already learned that guys are simple creatures. We like fatty foods and alcohol, plushy chairs and banal entertainment. We also *have* dicks, and this is the driving factor for a large percentage of everything else that we do in life, and this fact generates around us an aura of banality. Beauvoir also covers the psychoanalyst's perspective on woman, which she dismisses as ridiculous, since at the time the book was written the field was populated almost entirely by men, and due to the limitations of a system that bases its understanding of the broad range of human behavior on sexuality alone. Basically, penis-envy is bullshit.

Beauvoir covers the history of humanity in seventy-seven pages, so it's full of sweeping generalizations. Science has also uncovered much new information in the intervening years since this book's publication. Still, your D.O.D.'s fascinated by ancient civilizations, so I dorked out on these chapters. But I won't bore you with any in-depth analysis. All you need to do is refer to the above paragraph about men and their dicks to explain human history.

In Part III of Book I, Beauvoir discusses myths surrounding woman, perpetuated by the patriarchy. Kinsey, you may take note of your parents' forbiddance of the "spring break" ritual, for instance, as Beauvoir says, "Popular festivals today are still marked by outbursts of eroticism; woman appears here not simply as an object of pleasure, but as a means for attaining to that state of *hybris*, riotousness, in which the individual exceeds the bounds of self." So, there you go. No spring break for you, unless it involves the far less hedonistic endeavor of volunteering for Habitat for Humanity.

And as far as the myth of the empowerment of augmenting your body through plastic surgery goes: "The more the features and proportions of woman seem contrived, the more she rejoices the heart of man because she seems to escape the vicissitudes of natural things." Therefore, Kinsey, thou ought to think twice before thy cosmetic surgery.

About men and the myth of mothers-in-law, Beavoir says, "He loathes the thought that the woman he loves should have been engendered." I actually really love your G-Mama. Maybe she gets on my nerves sometimes, but she's great. If she reminds me again that she grew up on a farm in the South in the '60s I'm gonna kill her, but no, yeah, I totally love her.

And when it comes to actual myths in our culture, here's how lost your D.O.D. is at the time of this writing: you can make fun of my attempt to ban all things Disney. I'm sure my efforts will prove fruitless. But listen: "The Cinderella myth . . . flourishes especially in prosperous countries like America. How should the men there spend their surplus money if not upon a woman?" And is the Princess Industrial Complex a result of the prosperity of the 1990s? Have the riches of Internet burst and bust fallen out among primarily men, to be doled out to doting wives, hapless in submission? God, I hate the princess thing. And there are few worse than Cinderella, who sits around not doing shit for herself until some dude sweeps her foot up into a fragile slipper.

On D.H. Lawrence's *Lady Chatterley's Lover*, Beauvoir says, "Women should, like man, abdicate from all pride and self will; if she incarnates life for the man, so does he for her." Your mom and I will be the first to explain to you that we love each other, but in no way do we exemplify the above myth. Your mother is not my life, nor am I hers. For that matter, we don't live solely for you, either. Sorry if this comes as a shock, but life is much more than romance or sex or children. There's great music and museums, hiking through the woods, excellent beer. Divide yourself among those things you love. It's unhealthy to give yourself wholly to any one thing, including yourself.

Book II concerns itself with then-contemporary women's lives. Beauvoir starts with female babies and works her way through life up to old womanhood. This is the bulk of *The Second Sex*. There's a funny translator's note on page 296 about little girls and jeans ("The Formative Years: Childhood"): "Wearing jeans becomes distasteful for young women in America because they come "no nearer to manual labor than wielding a pen or riding a bicycle." How ironic that in this feminist text there could be so sweeping a generalization about American women, even for the 1950s! I'm beginning to understand some of those complaints about the translation. Kinsey, wearing jeans today has absolutely nothing to do with manual labor. In fact the last pair of jeans I purchased are too expensive for anything other than wearing out to dinner.

Beauvoir cites Liepman's *Jeunesse et sexualite* and quotes a number of young girls talking about their first knowledge of sex and reproduction, and all of them are crazy, as kids are wont to think of these things. Beauvoir claims—I would say correctly—that "even clear instruction would not solve the problem; with the best will in the world on the part of parents and teachers, it is impossible to put the erotic experience into words and concepts; it is to be comprehended only in living it." Nonetheless it's still valuable, I think, to leave open the lines of communication between children and parents when it comes to sex and having babies. Hopefully you'll agree that that was your experience, because I'm assuming that if you're reading this, you're not still confused. More importantly, let's talk about love: when I met your mom I thought she was very pretty. I know, you're squirming right now, but hear me out. Your mother's hair was a little longer than shoulder-length, thick and brown. She wore just a touch of makeup, maybe a little foundation and some eye shadow and mascara, a subtle lipstick. I've never been attracted to overly done-up women. I fell in love with your mom, and there's a difference between love and attraction. What we did on that first date was we talked, for hours. We kind of ate dinner (spaghetti and meatballs, which we made together in my apartment) but we were both a little too nervous—we liked each other too much—to eat. We talked about our families. It was a big deal to both of us that all of your grandparents were still married and always would be. That was a foundation for the kind of life we knew we were both searching for. That night we kissed. That was it. But I couldn't get the kiss out of my mind, and I called your mom the next day, and the next and the next, and we kept seeing each other. And that was the biggest part of making you. It's easy to be attracted to someone; love takes work. We kept going on dates, and for almost two weeks your mother was steadfast, no matter how hard I tried to—well, *you know*. If two weeks doesn't sound like a long time, then maybe you're reading this a little early. I won't bore you with the technical details of sex, since you've probably heard all about it by now. What matters is that your mom and I wanted to be with each other enough that we were hungry to know each other—not in a carnal way, but that way that makes you feel you're so close to someone that that person becomes an integral part of you, that if that person hurts it also hurts you, and if they're happy you're happy. That's what we wanted. I hope that when you read this, such a feeling still sparks between her and me. I have no doubt that it will.

Moving on through life, on the outset of menstruation, Beauvoir writes that a girl "does not yet grasp the significance of what is taking place in her. Her first menstruation reveals this meaning, and her feelings of shame appear." For my own part, I'll never forget Tanya Tomlinson's (who, incidentally, would become your D.O.D.'s first girlfriend) twelfth birthday party and this poor girl, Susan, I think her name was, got her period, maybe for the first time, and she was wearing a white skirt. All the girls disappeared into the bathroom with Susan for a long time. When they emerged, I saw Susan's stained skirt, though she tried to hide it underneath a sweatshirt tied around her waist. Tanya's grandmother had called Susan's mother to come pick her up. All of us boys who were at the party stood around wondering what to do. Feelings of shame and embarrassment emanated from Susan and the rest of the girls, though the grandmother told us it was normal, it was natural, and that we shouldn't make fun or laugh. Honestly, it was hard to know how to feel about any of it. It was, at that time, still a mystery to me. Some of the boys laughed though.

Around the middle of the book comes the "Sexual Initiation" chapter where Beauvoir writes, "Psychiatrists all agree on the extreme importance of a woman's first erotic experiences: their repercussions are felt throughout the rest of her life." This is definitely true, Kinsey, which is why your mom and I were so serious about your education, so that you would make healthy decisions, so that any "repercussions" might not be repercussions at all, that you might have a very positive relationship with your sexuality. Feeling weird yet? Well, in this chapter, the sexologist named Alfred Kinsey who conducted years of research in human sexuality gets a mention. This was my biggest impediment to our choice for your name. Your mom came up with your name, which she said sounded "cute," but "spunky," like you'd be full of energy. I just didn't want people to say, when they met you, "Like the sex guy?" Maybe you've already heard that, and if so, sorry. I hope you don't hate your name. I hated my name when I was a kid. I wanted to be a Jared, or a Mike, not Jamie. James sounded too old, or too formal or something. Some kids made fun of me because my name could be a girl's name. So, if you're plagued by Kinsey, maybe you could go by your middle name of Louise. In the end I agreed with your mom and we named you, because the name was not typical, and it does sound cute, but spunky. So far you have lived up to these adjectives. Your favorite thing to say is to tell me "no." You say, "No Daddy, this *my* arm," when I'm putting your arms through your shirt sleeves to get you dressed in the morning, for example.

And as far as sex goes, Beauvoir goes on, writing that, "To express the fact that he has copulated with a woman, a man says he has 'possessed' her, or he has 'had' her." Today, some of the language young men use for having had sex is much more violent. They might say that they "beat that pussy up," or use "smash" as a verb to describe the sex act, as in "I smash that last night." Never mind the error in past tense conjugation. This violent language is unsurprising in a culture that condones rape. I hope things will have changed for the better by the time you're reading this.

Beauvoir makes it sound like sex is never initiated by a woman, always by a man, and is generally unpleasant for women, which is fortunately not true for many people. And while I cannot say for certain what it's like for a woman to culminate in orgasm, Beauvoir talks about a man's ejaculation as being localized and finite, which is true—when talking about ejaculation. But she seems to equate ejaculation with orgasm, which leads me to think that old Sartre was doing it wrong.

On marriage: "Boys *get* married, they *take* a wife." Your Granny has on more than one occasion inquired if I asked your G-daddy and G-mama for permission to marry your mom, to which I laugh and explain that your grandparents probably would've said, "You don't know her very well, do you?" This perplexed Granny, and I had to explain that your mom would make up her own mind about marrying me or not, and she never would've agreed if I'd made the *faux pas* of asking anyone else for "permission" first. Granny has also mentioned that your uncle Bryan did ask your Aunty Julie's parents for permission, and this seems to be the preferable course of action, in Granny's POV.

Speaking of Granny, Beauvoir on the housewife and cleaning has this to say: "The maniac housekeeper wages her furious war against dirt, blaming life itself for the rubbish all living growth entails. . . . she loses *joie de vivre* . . . She becomes bitter and disagreeable and hostile to all that lives." This characterizes Granny perfectly, also your Aunty Megs! Unfortunately, I might be turning into that, too. Just ask your mom how crazy I'm driving her with my complaints about her dishes and teabags and other detritus strewn about our home. Beauvoir makes housework sound like the worst kind of unfulfilling drudgery. But at least here she does sound like she's writing about her contemporary time, and I very much picture a *Leave it to Beaver*-like scene with June being upset over Ward and the kids tracking mud on her shining kitchen floor. You'll probably have to do some research to understand that reference. But this hardly sounds like a 21st century home. And many people find great pleasure and fulfillment in keeping a tidy household, or in preparing excellent food (which is, of course, an art), and making a family feel secure. Beauvoir also says that children, even more than men, want to escape the confines of the household, which might be true at a certain point, but providing boundaries and stability is important: children especially crave it. They want to know that someone else is in charge. It doesn't have to be the woman, of course, and it's probably best if it's a joint effort on the part of both parents when possible. Beauvoir says, "there are many marriages that 'go well'—that is to say, in which man and wife reach a compromise. They live side by side without too much mutual torment." You probably won't have to look up what I mean when I say LOL.

Beauvoir goes into pregnancy, abortion, and motherhood. About abortion she says "Nothing could be more absurd than the arguments brought forward against the legalization of abortion." And here I agree, because even when abortion is outlawed, women still seek them, but under secrecy, which imposes poor, unclean, and/or dangerous conditions and no regulation. I don't know if you will continue to grow up in your current state of Georgia, but it isn't exactly warm to the idea of abortion. This country is full of people who can't for an instant think critically. They'll get all fired up about this, or about owning guns, and not give a second thought to the thousands dying in mostly unjustified wars. Just because abortion is legal doesn't mean that every woman's going to have one. For your part, I hope you make responsible decisions, and you already know that you'll have the support of your parents on whatever those choices are.

If you do get pregnant, Beauvoir says that your "body is at last [your] own, since it exists for the child who belongs to [you]." But according to my experience with your mother's pregnancy and your subsequent birth, breastfeeding, and weaning: upon this last stage your mother said, "Thank god, I get my body back." Your mom would claim that the most dependent she's ever felt was when she was chained to your survival. But don't let that get to you.

Beauvoir also covers what a woman's life is like in the social sphere, and what it's like for prostitutes, and what the ancient Greeks called *hetairas*, but which today we call celebrities. She talks about women getting "dressed up," and for some reason I couldn't help but think about one December when your mother and I visited San Francisco, and stayed in this nice, quaint bed and breakfast on Nob Hill. We had tickets to a Christmas show at the Symphony Orchestra, and I'd brought along my tuxedo, and your mom wore an elegant black dress. But when we left for the show, I decided we'd walk, not thinking about the fact that the most direct route would take us through the Tenderloin. People laughed at us, asking if we were lost, and asking for money. At one point I stepped over some poor soul laying on his back, half in the street and half on the sidewalk, moaning and retching in what looked like some agonizing drug and/or alcohol withdrawal. That was probably the most "dressed up" I've ever felt. I felt like some "guvnah" in a film adaptation of a Dickens novel.

Beauvoir goes into reasons why young girls enter into prostitution, including that their young lovers pressure them to do it. This makes me think of the memoir *Girlvert* by Oriana Small, a porn star who got into the business via pressure from her then-boyfriend, whom she loved.

Other reasons include familial or economic pressure, and here we are, Kinsey, living in the U.S.'s child sex trafficking capital: Atlanta. Your mom told me a story just the other day about a federal judge reviewing appeals cases of underage girls charged with prostitution. The judge declared that there's a serious problem when the legal age of consent in Georgia is sixteen, yet a thirteen-year-old has been charged with a sex crime. And what's up with the cultural phenomenon, especially in hip hop culture, for men to refer to themselves as pimps, usually meaning someone who's cool, stylish, and popular with the ladies, not usually a pimp in the literal sense. Still, the idea seems to come from the 1970s idea of a pimp, a guy who dresses garishly and wields power over "his bitches." The fact that such language exists tells us everything we need to know about contemporary male mentality when it comes to women. This language has infiltrated popular culture to the extent that it's no big deal to have a cable television show called *Pimp My Ride*, even if in this context "pimp" is a verb synonymous with "to decorate."

As for prostitutes and brothels, your D.O.D. for many years lived in Reno, Nevada, where, just outside of town, prostitution in brothels is legal. During pledge season in college, my fraternity "kidnapped" the pledge class president and made for the rest of the pledges a scavenger hunt that culminated at The Mustang Ranch, where the president and one of the active members sat at the bar drinking. I was once one of the active members who took the president to the cathouse. You rang a buzzer to get inside the gate, and when you entered the building (actually a trailer) the Madame had the prostitutes lined up for us to choose from. The prostitutes seemed pissed when we retreated to the bar, and for the rest of the night they'd sit next to us, and touch our thighs, and try to get us to buy them drinks, or to cajole us into the back rooms where they could discuss things like prices. If you're wondering if I ever *went there*, I suppose that would have to be another discussion.

At last Beauvoir goes into the life of the old woman, which is just as sad and debilitating as any other stage of life for woman that she describes. Quoting Phillip Wylie in *Generation of Vipers*, about American women's involvement in various social, cultural, political organizations, etcetera, the American woman, who "[Knows] nothing about medicine, art, science, religion, law, sanitation . . . seldom has any special interest in *what*, exactly, she is doing as a member of any of these endless organizations, so long as it is *something*." This makes me think of your G-mama, Kinsey. I couldn't even tell you how many different things she's involved in, from campaigning for the Democratic Party, to being a spokesperson at rallies for abused women, to her book club. The large exception, though, is that your G-mama holds a Master's degree and taught gifted students for years and is far from the ignorant mom that Beauvoir seems to be portraying.

Throughout the book, Kinsey, there's interesting and often startling information, like the woman who got off on her son breastfeeding to the point that "she had to fight the temptation to toy with his penis." Or a religious mystic who cleans up the waste of a man suffering from dysentery with her tongue. Another mystic drinks the water she used to wash lepers and feels a spiritual ecstasy, especially for the scale of leper skin she feels lodged in her throat. There are funny lines such as, "repressed women make shrewish wives, sadistic mothers, fanatical housekeepers, unhappy and dangerous creatures." Or the woman who gets "vexed if [her lover] does not live up to the image she has put in his place. If he gets tired or careless, if he gets hungry or thirsty at the wrong time, if he makes a mistake or contradicts himself, she asserts that he is 'not himself'" which reminded me of the parody of the Yuban commercial in *Airplane!*, where the woman thinks "Jim never has a second cup of coffee at home." You'll probably have to look up that reference, too.

But the biggest contention I have with the book is the foundation of existentialism on which the entirety of Beauvoir's argument sits. The famous sentence that begins Book II and reads, "One is not born, but rather becomes, a woman," follows from the existential argument that existence precedes essence. That is, you have to *act* before you can *be* anything. The problem with such an argument is clearly evident in her chapter on "The Lesbian," for Beauvoir assumes homosexuality to be a learned trait, and not an inherent one—just like the gender traits we apply to "woman." Funny enough, the other day someone I know was talking about his grandmother, who said she just couldn't understand why a gay person would choose to be that way, so he asked her what made her choose to be straight. Her response: "I didn't; I was just always that way." Clearly, who we are and what we become is some amazingly complicated algorithm of nature and nurture, and the absolute argument of existentialist thinking oversimplifies human life. I think of the *New York Times* reviewer of the 2010 translation who likewise pointed out that any parent who's seen his daughter gravitate immediately to the dolls, while ignoring the trucks and guns, or whatever, knows that some "feminine" traits are inherent and not learned.

But there's no argument about the state we're in and how important it is for you to know how to comport yourself in your life. Beauvoir writes that "How lively antifeminism still is can be judged by the eagerness of certain men to reject everything favorable to the emancipation of women." And in this time, Kinsey, there's ample evidence of such certain men, and women too. How people work to transcend their subjective selves seems to be through mutual love and respect. That's what Beauvoir keeps coming back to.

Beauvoir, at the time she wrote *The Second Sex*, equated mystical love and sexuality, in that the latter "is tinged with mysticism." She writes, "'My God, my adored one, my lord and master'—the same words fall from the lips of the saint on her knees and the loving woman on her bed; the one offers her flesh to the thunderbolt of Christ . . . the other, also, offers and awaits: thunderbolt, dart, arrow, are incarnated in the male sex organ." In order to transcend the trap of unequal love, what's need is "genuine love to be founded on the mutual recognition of two liberties." And this, ultimately, is how I leave you, darling daughter: however you choose to comport yourself is your choice and one that I will respect out of love, admiration, and respect for you.

Interestingly, throughout the book Beauvoir compares the position of the oppressed woman to that of African Americans in the United States. Ten years after this translation, Martin Luther King gave his "I Have a Dream" speech. Here we are in King's hometown. It is perhaps a historical irony that King talks about our nation one day achieving a "symphony of brotherhood," and that—in a linguistic irony—Beauvoir, too, ends *The Second Sex* by claiming that all humans will be free in a similar brotherhood, once woman is freed. Maybe when you read this, such arguments will seem quaint or antiquated. But when I think about the growing gap between rich and poor in our country and the lines of division that grow sharper between those who have access to equal rights and protections and those who do not, it seems more important than ever that a young woman like you should work to help those in less favorable conditions. I've always wanted to be a better man because of my girls, for my girls, for you and your mom, Kinsey. It's because of love that any of that is possible.

Don't forget it.
Love,
Dad

ACKNOWLEDGMENTS

Kevin Sampsell is a tireless supporter of the literary arts, someone whom I think is one of the most important writers, editors, and publishers in the English language today. I can't thank him enough for publishing this book, or for everything else he does for me and many others. Huge thanks, also, to the rest of the "team": Bryan Coffelt, who works wonders as a book designer; and Tina Morgan, for her great editorial eye. This book could not be without those first readers who helped me hone up this prose: Christopher Bundy, Blake Butler, and Man Martin. Thanks to my family: the Iredells and the Babcocks. Of course: Sarah Babcock and Kinsey Iredell.

JAMIE IREDELL

is originally from Monterey County, California, and now lives in Atlanta, where he writes and teaches writing to college students. He is the author of *Prose. Poems. a Novel.*, and *The Book of Freaks*. His stories, poems, and essays have appeared in many magazines, including *The Rumpus*, *PANK*, *Copper Nickel*, *The Literary Review*, *The Chattahoochee Review*, and *The Collagist*. He is fiction editor of *Atticus Review*.

www.ingramcontent.com/pod-product-compliance
Lightning Source LLC
Chambersburg PA
CBHW020928090426
42736CB00010B/1077